BEETHOVEN
Master Composer

Ludwig van Beethoven. (*Library of Congress*)

BEETHOVEN
Master Composer

HERBERT J. GIMPEL

Illustrated with Photographs

FRANKLIN WATTS

LONDON · NEW YORK

Franklin Watts Limited,
18 Grosvenor Street,
London, W.1.

TO RUTH

CONTENTS

BEETHOVEN
Master Composer

Bronze bust of Beethoven, at Beethoven-Haus, Bonn, West Germany. (Beethoven-Haus, Bonn)

PREFACE

This biography of Beethoven is the story of the man himself, not a treatise on his musical compositions. The great composer must therefore be placed in his everyday surroundings and viewed as a mortal man with all his human traits and weaknesses. In his unfamiliarity with the sophisticated ways of the world, Beethoven was often guileless and naïve. Because he concealed his finer qualities behind a blunt and crude manner, he was often misunderstood.

When Beethoven, because of his deafness, became sensitive and withdrew from society, he needed his music more than ever. It sustained him and gave him a sanctuary from the imagined injustices of friends and fortune. He found refuge in a creative world of tone, although he could hear his later works only in the realm of his masterful imagination. Through his indomitable spirit he emerged from his humble earthly surroundings to gain immortality as a composer.

Born a year after Napoleon, Beethoven lived in a changing world where the old ideas of royalty and aristocracy were being challenged by the revolutionary rumblings of independence, equality, and freedom. The American Declaration of Independence was signed when Beethoven was a lad of five, and the Bastille fell when he was a young man of eighteen.

Beethoven's early music was composed in the same traditional forms as that of Haydn, Bach, and Mozart. Later, however, Beethoven brought about a revolution in the world of music through his inspired creativity and bold genius. He always considered himself a king in the realm of music. As such, he assumed an equality to any king whom circumstance had placed upon a throne. The spirit of revolution that came at the close of the eighteenth century ushered in the nineteenth century with the promise of new freedom. Beethoven's musical creations reflected the times in which he lived. He dared to depart from the pleasant tonal patterns and pretty harmonies written to please the aristocracy.

Even before he became deaf, the great composer was denied the pleasure of hearing his symphonies played at their best. The orchestras of his time fell far short of the great symphony orchestras of today, which present Beethoven's music closer to the perfection he strove for. It is a great wonder that a deaf composer could create such lasting masterpieces of music.

To approach a subject such as the life of Beethoven is an awe-inspiring task, for the writer has the feeling of treading on hallowed ground. A personal visit to the places Beethoven made famous, from his birthplace at Bonn to his grave in Vienna, does nothing to dispel the awe. On the Bonngasse is the charming Beethoven-Haus, where the composer was born on the third floor in a little garret room. On display are his old ear trumpets, stringed instruments, and an ancient organ he played as a child.

The Fischer house, where young Ludwig was raised, is now gone, and a new neighborhood has sprung up to replace the old. From there, one can still see the Rhine River with its fascinating cargo boats. Looming in the distance, beyond the Rhine, are the mountains that Beethoven gazed on as a boy.

The huge cathedral still rises above the chimneys and rooftops of Bonn. Here young Beethoven played the organ, and the impressive church music resounded through the high-vaulted arches of stone. A part of Beethoven's world is still in Bonn two centuries after his birth. He left his stamp on the city, and his music and spirit still seem to pervade the streets.

A search for the many places where Beethoven lived in and around Vienna involves miles of walking and endless questions. Many of his former dwelling places are marked with plaques and flags to guide persistent pilgrims of history.

In everyday life, Europeans live so intimately with history that a delicatessen or a cobbler's shop may now occupy the site where a stirring event took place, or cows may graze peacefully on a former battlefield. On the fourth floor above the humble shops in the Pasqualati house on the Mölkerbastei are Beethoven's former lodgings. Here one of his old pianos still stands in quiet dignity. The view from his old rooms is well worth the walk up the winding stone stairs.

At a gay café in Heiligenstadt, families gather to enjoy a buffet, music, and the new wine from the surrounding vineyards while they sit under the grape arbors for an evening of pleasant sociability. Well-worn stone stairs lead to Beethoven's room, where he lived during a country sojourn from Vienna. His room cannot be visited, however, because the chef now lives there.

Throughout the research and writing of this book, my wife, Ruth, proved once again her secretarial proficiency. In addition to her editing and typing chores she took notes on the many places we visited as we walked miles over cobblestones, through alleyways and strange neighborhoods in Bonn, Vienna, and nearby villages.

Since much of the material on Beethoven was originally translated from the German, some of the quotations have been changed for clarity while the meaning has been carefully preserved. I would like to acknowledge the kind assistance of a few of the many people who proved most helpful. Professor Joseph Schmidt-Görg, an eminent authority on Beethoven, was good enough to share part of his vast knowledge to guide this foreign stranger to the important places that were a part of Beethoven's life in Bonn.

In Vienna, I was given invaluable assistance by Hofrat Dr. Hans Pauer and Fräulein Salm of the Austrian National Library. Fräulein Salm's knowledge of the available Beethoven material in Vienna saved days of hunting. Other organizations to which I am indebted are the Library of Congress; the libraries of Washington, D.C., and Naples, Florida; the British Museum in London; and the Beethoven-Haus in Bonn.

No book can be considered a suitable monument for that great immortal of music, Beethoven. He needs none, for his music is monument enough to immortalize him from the past to eternity.

Herbert J. Gimpel
Naples, Florida

ONE

"He Will Become a Great Man"

The stubby little fingers of a six-year-old boy ran over the keys of an old clavichord, playing the simple exercises with almost mechanical perfection. He was such a little fellow, even for his age, that he had to stand on a footstool to reach the keys. Under his mop of black hair the tears streamed down his cheeks, for he was compelled by his father to practice hour after hour. The father insisted that his little boy play the notes rapidly and flawlessly; he hoped that as a child prodigy his son would win fame, money, and admiration. This brilliant child who showed such great promise was Ludwig van Beethoven.

Born in poverty and obscurity, Ludwig seemed to have little prospect of making a name for himself. The wailing cry of a newborn infant had announced his birth in an atticlike room dimly lit by a dormer window

The house where Beethoven was born in a garret room on the third floor. (Beethoven-Haus, Bonn)

on the third floor of a house on the Bonngasse in Bonn, Germany. The sound died away quickly and was so little thought of at the time that no one is quite sure whether it was heard on the sixteenth or the seventeenth of December in the year 1770. Still, that birth cry marked the arrival of a tiny baby who would one day change the world of music.

Ludwig's grandfather had moved to Bonn in 1733. He was of Flemish stock, the son of a baker in Flanders. According to the blurred history, Archbishop Clemens August, Elector of Cologne, heard that a twenty-one-year-old church singer named Beethoven had a fine voice and was well trained in music. The Elector of Cologne asked the young man to enter his service. That is how the Beethovens came to settle in Bonn, then a pleasant, peaceful city of ten thousand people on the banks of the Rhine.

In ancient times, Bonn had been leveled by the barbarians, and near the end of the ninth century it was once more destroyed in a raid by Norsemen who rowed up the Rhine by boat. The successive electors, or rulers, of Cologne had resided in Bonn since 1265, until the chain of succession was broken in Beethoven's day. Conquered by Napoleon, Bonn fell under the yoke of the French and later became a part of Prussia by decree of the Congress of Vienna. Today it is the capital of West Germany, and is a beautiful, thriving city of about 150,000 people.

As a young man, Beethoven's grandfather, also

named Ludwig van Beethoven, married a local girl, Maria Josepha. As organist and choir singer in the palace he rose quickly in the service of the Archbishop Elector. Later, this Beethoven became the director of the orchestra, with the title of *Kapellmeister*. The responsibilities of marriage prompted him to augment his income by investing in the rich Rhine vineyards and the wine business that flourished around Bonn.

With his marriage to Josepha, his musical career, and his interest in the wineries, one might think that the *Kapellmeister*'s life would have been a happy one. Such was not the case, however. Of the three children born to Josepha and the *Kapellmeister*, only one survived—a boy named Johann. After the misfortune of losing her other children early in life, Josepha evidently sought escape by imbibing freely of the wines that were so readily available. When her husband, Ludwig, died at the age of sixty-one, Josepha became a pitiful alcoholic. During her last years she was placed in a nearby convent.

Johann van Beethoven was given every opportunity to develop his musical ability and, like his father, was employed by the Elector to sing in the choir and play in the orchestra. He was destined never to rise above mediocrity in the musical arts and was kept in the employ of the Elector, Maximilian Friedrich, primarily because of his talented father, the *Kapellmeister*. Johann was endowed with handsome features, abundant vanity, and in his later life, an overdeveloped thirst for wine. In general, he seems to have acquired the characteristics of his mother rather than those of his father.

At the age of twenty-seven, Johann married a widow, twenty-one-year-old Maria Magdalena Laym, the daughter of the head chef in one of Bonn's castles. When she was born to the Kewerich family, her birth marked the beginning of a luckless life. She married Johann Laym when she was barely seventeen. Their only child died in infancy. Less than three years after their marriage her husband died.

Soon thereafter, Maria married Johann van Beethoven. She was remembered as a soft-spoken, gentle, hard-working girl who led a cheerless existence. She had much to be sad about. Johann, her handsome husband, was inadequately educated and a poor provider. He often arrived home drunk and disturbingly noisy. His irresponsibility accounted in part for the family's extreme poverty and made it difficult for poor Maria to manage the household. Her naturally amiable nature was always shadowed by the melancholy and long-suffering of a wife and mother vainly trying to make ends meet.

"What is marriage?" she once remarked to a neighbor. "A little joy followed by a chain of sorrows."

Maria and Johann's first child to survive infancy was named Ludwig after his grandfather. The *Kapellmeister* and little Ludwig formed a strong bond of affection. Unfortunately, the dearly beloved grandfather died on

Christmas Eve when Ludwig was only three years old. After the old man's death the family finances grew steadily worse.

In the meantime, the family grew, and eventually there were five mouths to feed. Ludwig was four years older than his brother Karl and six years older than his youngest brother, Johann. Unhappily, their father's thirst for wine increased with the size of his family. Little Ludwig, sensitive and serious, watched his mother struggle to hold the miserable family together while his father enjoyed his tavern friends, oblivious to the suffering of his impoverished wife and children.

Sympathizing with his mother, Ludwig became sad and silent as he held within him all his feelings of outraged shame. His brooding, introspective nature developed at an age when he should have been laughing and playing with the other children of Bonn.

Young Ludwig was described by Doctor Müller, a neighbor, as "a shy and taciturn boy, the necessary consequence of the life apart which he led, observing more and pondering more than he spoke, and disposed to abandon himself entirely to the feelings awakened by music."

Shortly after Ludwig's birth his family had moved to a house owned by the Fischer family in the Rheingasse. Gottfried Fischer was a master baker who died too soon to know the fame that Ludwig would one day bring to his old house. After Beethoven's death, many people visited Bonn to see the place where the famous composer had spent his early childhood. Many thought that the Fischer house was Ludwig's birthplace, and the Fischer family, enjoying the fame brought to their home, did nothing to dispel the illusion.

The Fischers recorded many memories of Ludwig, the stocky little fellow with the swarthy skin and the unruly head of hair, during those early days in Bonn. They told of his lessons under Herr Huppert at the elementary school and his later attendance at the Münsterschule.

Although Johann was not a great musician himself, he was determined to make one of his son. The chance of developing another breadwinner in the family appealed to him and he decided to capitalize on Ludwig's natural musical talent. Mozart, Johann's idol, was fourteen years older than Ludwig and had set a glittering example of concert brilliance at the piano as well as in his compositions. At nineteen, Mozart had already composed symphonies, chamber music, operas, concertos, and many other musical works.

Ludwig was scolded, punished, and forced to practice on the clavier and violin when he would much rather have run down to the banks of the Rhine to watch the river barges go by. One of Johann's singing and drinking companions recalled that he and Ludwig's father would often come home late at night from the tavern, get the tiny fellow out of bed, and keep him playing at the clavier until morning.

Johann was so obsessed with making his son a competent musician that Ludwig had little time left for his school studies. As a result, he did poorly in school. His father concentrated on the talented Ludwig, for his other sons, Karl and Johann, showed little musical promise.

In time, Ludwig began playing his own melodies instead of his written music lessons. His father would not tolerate such dawdling.

"What nonsense are you scratching together again?" he asked. "You are not to do that yet. Apply yourself to the piano and violin. Strike the notes quickly and accurately. That is more important."

When young Ludwig was eight, his father arranged a concert in Cologne for him and a young contralto. Johann billed his son as a six-year-old in order to make him appear more of a child prodigy. The success of the concert is left in doubt. The newspaper read simply: "The young lady sang arias and the little boy of six years played clavier concertos and trios."

Occasionally Johann, along with several other musicians, would give a concert in his home. He was very proud of his son's musical ability.

"My son Ludwig," he said, "is now my only joy. He is getting on so well in music and composition, everyone looks upon him with great admiration. My Ludwig—I can see that in time he will become a great man in the world. You who are gathered here, and live to see it, remember my words!"

Gottfried Fischer, the landlord, who had to arise very early in the morning to bake bread, found these home concerts annoying.

"If I were not a baker," he informed Johann, "all this disturbance from outsiders would not worry me. One has the night for rest. But, as I am a baker and must stay up at night to bake, I must sleep in the daytime. I cannot stand it. It will ruin my health. Herr van Beethoven, I am sorry to tell you that you must look for other lodgings." Nevertheless, the Beethovens were allowed to stay on at the Fischer house.

Having taught his son as much as he could, Johann realized that he would have to look elsewhere for further and better instruction. Tobias Pfeiffer, a court tenor, gave Ludwig music lessons for a brief time, and the aged court organist Van den Eeden showed him the intricate workings of the organ. Ludwig was still such a little fellow that he could barely reach the pedals. This difficulty, however, did not diminish his interest. He made friends with Friar Willibald Koch, the organist at the local Franciscan monastery, and with Zenser, the organist at the Münster church in Bonn.

Ludwig soon gained proficiency under the teaching of Van den Eeden and occasionally substituted for him at the organ. He became highly skilled at improvising on preludes and accompaniments, to the amazement of the other musicians and singers. He was soon playing the organ for early mass at six o'clock every morning at the Minorite monastery.

However gifted Ludwig was, his instruction had not been thorough or systematic. Fortunately, a fine organist and composer, thirty-one-year-old Christian

The steeples of the Münster church in Bonn, where Beethoven played the organ as a youth. (H. J. Gimpel)

Gottlob Neefe, arrived from Leipzig. The stoop-shouldered Neefe was exactly what eight-year-old Ludwig needed to advance his musical training.

Neefe brought with him some of the sonatas of Karl Philipp Emanuel Bach, son of the great composer Johann Sebastian Bach. Mozart had played some of the younger Bach's music in concert and considered him one of the greatest of musicians. Neefe also brought with him the *Well-tempered Clavier*, by Johann Sebastian Bach. It was in manuscript form, since it had not been published at that time. When it was published years later, it appeared in two volumes. Each volume included twenty-four preludes and fugues for each of the major and minor keys.

The difficult and intricate *Well-tempered Clavier* was given to the boy as a major project in his lessons. Under Neefe's patient teaching, Ludwig's stubby little fingers soon were rippling confidently through the preludes and fugues. His fast progress and mastery of the lengthy composition impressed his teacher, who liked Ludwig's "forceful and finished" playing. The lad entered into every changing mood of the composition, from its brooding movements and harmonies to its joyous rapid passages.

Neefe helped develop Ludwig toward his full potential as a concert pianist and organist.

"If I ever become a great man," Beethoven said to Neefe, "you shall have a share of the credit."

From his attic room, Ludwig could hear the carillon in

the bell tower of the Elector's palace. He learned to love the sounds pealing across the peaceful town. His heart always quickened to their music, and the memories they awakened stayed with him always. The friendly clang of church bells eased his loneliness and spoke to him across the city. While he walked in the country, the bells vibrated over the fields from a distant village. Until he could hear no more, the song of the birds, the babbling of a brook, the wind stirring through the trees, and the tolling of the bells remained treasured sounds in his life. Beethoven later tried to capture all these sounds and transform them into musical creations.

There is little wonder that Ludwig, saddened by a tyrannical father and a tragically sorrowful mother, had to look outside his home for a few moments of stolen happiness. The melodies of the bells and the river flowing by were two of his most pleasant memories, even though they were associated with tragedy.

Ludwig remembered the year when the Rhine went on a rampage, flooding the low-lying areas of Bonn. As the swirling water rose around the Beethoven home, Ludwig's mother proved her character. She remained behind so long to help others flee that she finally had to make her own escape by climbing over boards and ladders. When the water receded, it left mud and destruction in the houses of Bonn.

Ludwig also remembered the morning when a disastrous fire broke out in the archbishop's palace. Racing quickly through the great rooms, the fire soon spread to the powder magazine under the tower. When the tower crumbled, the carillon bells crashed to the ground, their music silenced as they lay in tragic disarray amid the charred ruins.

It is not surprising that Ludwig became moody and brooded more than a young lad should, for life's pleasures always seemed to him to be accompanied by sorrow.

Ludwig's round face and tousled black hair could at times be seen framed in the little attic window as he looked out across the Rhine onto a wondrous world of mystery. He could see the mountains in the distance on the other side of the river, and at night the stars suggested the vast infinity of creation.

As the river flowed along, Ludwig watched the boats and barges gliding by to places he had never seen—past the houses scattered along the green banks, the vineyards on the hills, and the storybook castles. Looking out the window, he did not realize that he would one day capture the pulse of the universe in tones and rhythms.

TWO

"*He Will Give the World Something To Talk About*"

Ludwig soon learned that success, money, and advancement were not easily attained, even for a lad willing to spend long hours in exhausting practice. When the old court organist Van den Eeden died, Neefe was appointed to take his place. Eleven-year-old Ludwig became his helper. He played during choir rehearsals and occasionally substituted for Neefe. Nevertheless, he still was not recognized as part of the Elector's establishment.

At the age of twelve, Ludwig was officially appointed as deputy cembalist. (The cembalist was a harpsichord player.) He was now authorized to wear the livery of the Elector. The lad must have cut a slightly comical figure with his short, stocky figure decked out in the pretentious finery of a court musician, described by a neighbor of the Fischer family as "a sea-green frock coat,

The old organ which Beethoven played as a youth. (Beethoven-Haus, Bonn)

green knee breeches with buckles, stockings of white or black silk, shoes with black bows, embroidered waistcoat with pocket flaps and bound with genuine gold cord. His hair was curled and with a queue, a soft hat was held under his left arm, and a sword was carried on his left side with a silver belt.''

Comical or not, Ludwig certainly earned his right to wear the uniform. He accompanied the singers and conducted the court orchestra during rehearsals. By assisting the *Kapellmeister* and the organist, he gained experience in orchestral, vocal, and keyboard music—wonderful training for a young musician.

Original melodies were always welling up in young Ludwig's head. Realizing this, Neefe gave him the project of writing three variations on a march by Ernst Christoph Dressler. As usual, Ludwig surprised his teacher with his talent. Instead of three variations, he wrote nine, all of them well done. Neefe proudly sent an article to one of the musical journals telling about his remarkable young student and his ''most promising talent.''

''This youthful genius is deserving of help to enable him to travel. He would surely become a second Wolfgang Amadeus Mozart were he to continue as he has begun.''

The variations on Dressler's march marked a significant beginning for Beethoven. He shortly followed them with three piano sonatas—melodies and themes of his own origin—and dedicated them to the aged Archbishop and Elector of Cologne, Maximilian Friedrich, who still resided in his big white palace at Bonn.

Ludwig had been working without pay while he so ably served his apprenticeship. When he was thirteen, he petitioned the Elector for official recognition as assistant court organist. The request was approved, but because the coffers were then short of funds the salary was not established. When the old archbishop died, Ludwig was left without a penny for his years of musical effort.

The situation soon improved under the new Elector of the Bishopric of Cologne, Maximilian Franz. He was the youngest son of Empress Maria Theresa of Austria, Hungary, and Bohemia. Maria Theresa was the mother of Marie Antoinette—queen to Louis XVI, king of France—and of Marie Caroline, queen of Naples. An older son was the ruler of Modena, a province of Italy.

In order to fill the dual role of Elector and Archbishop, twenty-eight-year-old Maximilian Franz took a three-week course at a seminary in Cologne to remedy his lack of theological knowledge and qualify him to wear the robes of an archbishop.

Maximilian Franz was a great patron of the arts and sciences, a lover of music, and a ruler who made Bonn a center of culture. The intellectual atmosphere was a favorable one for young Beethoven to work in and further his development as a musician and composer. He played the violin in the court orchestra and later became the principal cembalist. In the orchestra he became good friends with the violinist Franz Ries and the French-horn player Nicolaus Simrock. He was introduced to the best music of his day, and in his spare time read many of the works of Shakespeare, Lessing, Goethe, and Schiller. As Bonn flourished in cultural activity, Ludwig's artistic talent steadily developed.

An early visitor to the court at Bonn described Beethoven as "wanting in nothing which goes to make the great artist. All the superior performers of this orchestra are his admirers. They are all ears when he plays, but the man himself is exceedingly modest and without pretension of any kind."

Ludwig's home atmosphere offered very little except sadness and poverty. When Ludwig was fifteen, his little sister, Maria Margaretha Josepha, was born. The Beethovens could ill afford to feed another mouth. Ludwig loved his weary mother and infant sister. Even though he had little affection for his two younger brothers, Karl and Johann, he felt a responsibility in helping to feed them. Ludwig's sad expression often reflected his shame over the conduct of his heavy-drinking father.

To earn extra money, Ludwig gave music lessons to the children of the von Breuning family. It was in their home that he was introduced to a happy family life, good manners, and intellectual pleasures. Madame von Breuning had lost her husband in a fire at the Elector's palace and now was devoting herself to raising her four children with love, grace, and understanding. At the von

Breunings, Ludwig found these wonderful qualities in abundance. There he also met Madame von Breuning's friend Count Waldstein.

"Her home was pervaded by an atmosphere of unconstrained refinement," Franz Wegeler, a friend, later wrote of Madame von Breuning. "The useful and agreeable were found combined in the little social entertainments of family friends. It was not long before Beethoven was treated as one of the children. He spent the greater part of the day in Madame von Breuning's home, and not infrequently the night. He felt at home in the family, and everything around him contributed to cheer him and to develop his mind."

Neefe was so pleased with Ludwig's hard work and amazing genius that he petitioned the Elector to appoint the lad his assistant court organist. Maximilian Franz gladly signed the document of appointment, which included a list of Beethoven's duties.

On all Sundays and regular festivals, High Mass at 11 A.M. and vespers at 3 or 4 P.M. The vespers to be sung throughout in *Capellis Solemnibus* by the musicians of the electoral court—the middle vespers to be sung by the court clergy and musicians chorally as far as the "Magnificat," which will be performed musically.

On all Wednesdays in Lent the "Miserere" will be sung in the chapel at 5 P.M. and on all Fridays the "Stabat Mater."

Every day throughout the year two Masses will be read, the one at 9 A.M. and the other at 11 A.M.—on Sundays the latter at 10.

By now, Ludwig had far surpassed his father in musical ability and was free to experiment on the keyboard with his original preludes and improvisations. He could play beautifully, with great variation, at the organ or piano. Although he could sight-read very well, he delighted in following musical flights of his own fancy.

Ludwig was fortunate in having Maximilian Franz as the Elector of Cologne at Bonn. Maximilian Franz was a fat, jolly, intelligent, and well-educated archduke who played the viola fairly well and had a large library of music. He established the fine university at Bonn, created the botanical garden, and opened a free reading room in the palace library. He was an excellent ruler and administrator; because of Napoleon's conquests he was to be the last Elector of Cologne.

Maximilian Franz recognized Ludwig's talents, and with the encouragement of Neefe, authorized and paid for the lad's visit to Vienna and Mozart. Sixteen-year-old Ludwig climbed up to his seat on a post coach and headed for the musical mecca of Europe. Traveling by way of Munich, he finally reached Vienna.

The young musician's visit was neither long nor well recorded. Anton Schindler, later his friend and voluntary secretary, wrote that two people impressed young Beethoven. One was Joseph II, the Emperor of Austria, and the other was Mozart. The accounts of the meeting with Mozart are clouded by time and telling. One of Mozart's biographers, Otto John, wrote:

Beethoven, who was a very promising young man, came to Vienna in the spring of 1787. He was taken to see Mozart, who asked him to play for him, which he did. Mozart, believing that he was listening to a well-prepared composition, praised it rather coolly. Beethoven, aware of this, asked Mozart to give him a theme for improvisation. He always played his best when put to a test and now, inspired by the presence of the master whom he greatly respected, Beethoven began to play.

Mozart's attention and interest grew more and more. At length, he went quietly to some friends sitting in the adjoining room and said emphatically, "Keep your eyes on this fellow. Someday he will give the world something to talk about."

Beethoven's visit to Vienna and the great Mozart was cut all too short, for, two months after his arrival, he received a letter from his father urging him to hurry back to Bonn because his mother was extremely ill. Beethoven had traveled only halfway back from Vienna when his money ran out. He was forced to borrow from a family friend in order to continue his journey to his mother's bedside. All the while, he was extremely worried that he would not arrive in time.

Young Beethoven playing before Mozart and the elite of Viennese society. (Oesterreichische Nationalbibliothek, Vienna)

When he reached Bonn and home, he was heartsick. His mother was barely alive. Next to her bed in a cradle was his tiny baby sister, so sick that no one could tell which of the two might die first.

Some of the household goods had been pawned to raise money for survival. The house itself, without the mother's long-suffering drudgery, was a shambles; every room was dirty and disheveled. Ludwig's younger brothers were of no help whatsoever, and his father had resorted to the wineglass far too liberally in trying to soften the hideous realities of his pitiful life.

Maria Magdalena died in July, and her infant daughter, Maria Margaretha, followed her in November. This was the climax of an unhappy homelife for young Ludwig, who had been his mother's only ray of hope and joy during her last sad years on earth.

Ludwig wrote a letter to the friend who had kindly loaned him the money to complete his journey home.

The nearer I came to my hometown, the more letters reached me from my father, urging me to hurry, as my mother was not in good health. Although far from well myself, I hurried on with all possible speed. The desire to be able to see my dying mother overcame every obstacle. I found her still alive, but in a deplorable condition. She was ill with tuberculosis, and about seven weeks ago, after suffering much pain, she died.

She was a kind and lovable mother to me, and

my best friend. I hope to obtain your forgiveness for my long silence. As for the extreme kindness you showed me in Augsburg in lending me three carolins, I must beg you to please be indulgent with me a little longer. My journey has been a great expense and there is little hope of earning extra money in this place. Fate is not kind to me here in Bonn.

The Beethovens continued in dire financial straits during these gloomy months. Even the mother's cemetery plot was not fully paid for. To save money, the body of an Italian priest was interred in the same grave. Over a century passed before poor Maria Magdalena's bones were finally exhumed and she was given a grave of her own. Carved on her headstone is her name and the words of her illustrious son: "She was a kind and lovable mother to me, and my best friend."

At seventeen, Ludwig shouldered the responsibility of providing for his drunken father and his two brothers, Karl and Johann. Ludwig paid for their cheap quarters in the Wenzelgasse and for the housekeeper who cooked for them. Since his father was no longer of any value as a musician in the court, the Elector dismissed him. The genial Maximilian Franz, however, ordered half of Johann's salary to be paid to Ludwig, "besides the salary which he now draws and the three measures of grain for the support of his brothers."

In this manner Ludwig supported his family for over

five years. He had hoped that his brother Karl would take music lessons and become proficient enough to gain a place in the court orchestra, but Karl showed little promise. Ludwig's youngest brother, Johann, inherited no spark of musical talent and was finally apprenticed to the court apothecary, to learn the art of dispensing drugs.

When the boys' father died, shortly after Beethoven left Bonn permanently, no one mourned. The only mark of regret recorded over his passing was that of the good-natured Elector, Maximilian Franz, who remarked: "The liquor excise taxes have suffered a loss."

Ludwig had seen more than his share of the cruel and miserable side of life during his early years. Denied the carefree pleasures of childhood, he was forced to assume a man's responsibility at an early age. His circumstances left their stamp on his personality, but they made a man of him.

The von Breuning family continued as a source of inspiration and happiness to him during his last years in Bonn. Christoph, the oldest brother, was a law student. Eleonore was an attractive teen-ager, also called Lorchen. Stephan, younger than Ludwig, studied music with him and became a lifelong friend. The youngest boy of the family was Lorenz, nicknamed Lenz. Ludwig gave all the children piano lessons, but he particularly enjoyed teaching Lorchen.

Madame von Breuning recognized Ludwig's great talent as well as his need for motherly affection. She provided some badly needed exposure to good manners. In addition, the lad was introduced to the classics of Plutarch and Homer, translated from the Greek. From Plutarch, Beethoven learned of Homer's courage and heroism in carrying on with great dignity in spite of his blindness. The thought of Homer may have helped sustain Beethoven when deafness later threatened to shut him off from the world socially and musically.

His visits to the von Breuning family changed Ludwig. He became less blunt, overcame his shyness, and learned to pay more attention to his dress and personal cleanliness. The years of stark poverty and relentless struggle left their mark, however, and at times he would slip into a morose mood. When a brooding spell overcame him, Madame von Breuning understood, and excused him by saying, "Ludwig is in a *raptus* [trance]." During his entire life, Beethoven never forgot this fine, understanding woman. He referred to her as his guardian angel.

It was only natural that Ludwig should fall in love with pretty Eleonore. His infatuation for Lorchen proved to be only the first of a long series of disappointments in love. She later married Franz Wegeler, who became a medical doctor and a professor of medicine.

During these last years in Bonn, Ludwig's musicianship improved and he enjoyed his position as court organist and cembalist in the Elector's palace. He also played a viola in the orchestra which, through the interest of Maximilian Franz, became one of the finest in Europe.

This was one of the more enjoyable periods of Beethoven's life.

A friendly fellow among those who knew him, Ludwig loved to laugh at a good joke as well as anyone, and he had a broad sense of humor. In spite of the image he often invokes of a genius with a tempest inside, shaking his fist at the gods of fate, he had a tender heart. He was particularly well liked by his fellow musicians, for he had developed into a great pianist with an inspiring personality. One visitor to Bonn, having heard Beethoven play, glowed with enthusiasm over the young musician's "almost inexhaustible wealth of ideas, the altogether characteristic style of expression, and the great execution he displays."

One of the lifelong friendships Beethoven gained during these years was that of Count Ferdinand Waldstein. The count had come to Bonn from Austria to be made a Knight of the Teutonic Order by the Elector, who was grand master of the order. Waldstein was an amateur musician, and immediately felt a strong liking for Beethoven. He visited almost daily to play with him or just to listen as his new friend's fingers flew over the keyboard.

The count bought a new piano for his gifted friend, for Beethoven's old instrument was pitifully inadequate for his genius. Waldstein managed to give the young musician some extra income under the pretext that it came from the Elector, and he commissioned Beethoven to write a ballet that he could present at court. This work, the *Ritterballet*, when first performed, was thought to be a musical creation of the count's. It was later acknowledged as a composition of Beethoven's.

It was probably the count who convinced Ludwig to go to Vienna to study under Franz Joseph Haydn. Beethoven prevailed upon the Elector to give him a leave of absence on full salary. His days at Bonn were quickly drawing to a close. The French Revolution was boiling in France and threatened to engulf the rest of Europe. The Elector's sister, Marie Antoinette, and Louis XVI had been caught trying to escape from France the year before, in 1791, and they were now prisoners of the country they had once ruled.

The armies of France were already advancing toward Austria and Italy. In the spring of 1792, France declared war on Austria. By October, French soldiers were massing along the Rhine, and refugees were arriving in Bonn. A local militia was formed to protect the town; the Elector's treasury was moved to Düsseldorf for safekeeping. Maximilian Franz would soon be forced to depart ahead of the advancing French legions. There was little time to think of music now, and Beethoven's services as organist would not be needed in this time of crisis.

Beethoven packed his belongings for an early departure in the darkness of a November morning. Once again he climbed up to his seat in the post coach, to leave Bonn and the joys and sorrows of the first twenty-one years of his life. Riding along in the swaying coach, he passed the little houses scattered along the banks of the Rhine and drew away from the bittersweet memories of his youth. For him, the door closed forever on the quaint city where he had grown to manhood and where he had developed into a fine musician.

Later Beethoven described his Rhineland home to Wegeler as "my fatherland, the beautiful region in which I first saw the light—still clear and beautiful before my eyes."

Ahead lay fame and Beethoven's great years as a musician and composer. He did not leave sorrow and trouble behind; they were to follow him always. A new phase of his life was about to begin in Vienna, a city he would help make the capital of the world of music.

THREE

"*You Shall Receive the Spirit of Mozart from the Hands of Haydn*"

When Beethoven left his hometown in 1792 he was the most talented musician in Bonn. Mozart, the world's greatest musical prodigy, had died when he was only thirty-five, almost a year before Beethoven returned to Vienna. Ending his days in poverty and obscurity, Mozart was buried without ceremony in a pauper's unmarked grave. Franz Joseph Haydn then became the greatest living composer and the dean of musicians in Vienna.

Packed in Beethoven's luggage when he left Bonn was a farewell album given to him by his many friends. Count Waldstein's parting message read:

Mozart, Haydn, and Beethoven—three composers who lived in Vienna almost contemporaneously. (Oesterreichische National-bibliothek, Vienna)

Dear Beethoven:

You are going to Vienna to fulfill your long-frustrated wishes. By unceasing hard work you shall receive the spirit of Mozart from the hands of Haydn.

Beethoven had met Haydn before, when "old Papa Haydn" had visited Bonn. The old composer had heard Beethoven play and was well aware of his great ability as a musician. Since the young Rhinelander was already a virtuoso on the piano, Haydn was to become his teacher in composition.

Vienna was destined to be Beethoven's permanent home. The French soon swallowed up the Rhineland, and the Elector, Maximilian Franz, fled before their armies.

Beethoven arrived in Vienna with good credentials, and introductions to the finest of Viennese society. Prince Karl Lichnowsky, who had been a patron of Mozart's, was a great lover of music. He welcomed young Beethoven into his palatial home to give concerts for his friends. Fine music was a luxury that only the wealthy could afford, and affluent patronage was needed for it to flourish. The wealthy Viennese were enchanted by good music, and small concerts were a favorite form of entertainment. Many of the amateur musicians of the day were noblemen and ladies with titles.

Young Beethoven immediately found a place in this

gay, music-loving society. In a short time he gained the admiration of the Viennese by his remarkable brilliance as a piano virtuoso. His mastery of improvisation on any given musical theme won him fame and a comfortable living.

It became necessary for the somewhat rustic young man from Bonn to buy some new clothes in order to move about in the polite society that now lionized him.

"I must buy an entirely new outfit," he jotted down in his notebook.

He listed the prices he paid for his silk stockings and shoes. He wrote down the address of a dancing teacher who might instruct him in the social graces. The brilliant dexterity of his fingers on the keyboard, however, steadfastly refused to extend to his feet. It is amazing that a person with such mastery of rhythm at the piano never could manage to engage his feet in time to the cadence of a simple dance. It also seems strange that the great Beethoven could not carry a tune. Apparently it was only in his mind and on paper that his musical tones rang true.

Beethoven always paused before beginning a concert and waited for the animated chatter of his sophisticated audience to subside. His humble home at Bonn seemed far away as he gazed at the colorful assemblage in the salons of Vienna. Settling down to hear his first opening chords were refined gentlemen wearing soft velvet jackets, and ladies in long flowing gowns of silk and satin. Jewelry sparkled in the candlelight, and the scent of perfumes pervaded the room.

Beethoven's pupil Karl Czerny wrote of the piano virtuoso's playing: "His improvisation was very brilliant, astonishing in the highest degree. No matter in what society he was thrown, he made such an impression on all his listeners that it frequently happened that not a dry eye was to be seen, while many broke into sobs. There was something wonderful in his expression besides the beauty and originality of his ideas and the highly sophisticated way he had of presenting them. When he finished an improvisation of this kind he would burst into laughter and poke fun at his listeners over the emotions he had excited."

The many tedious hours he had spent practicing his lessons under the relentless demands of his father were now proving to be hours well spent. A happy, carefree child with a room cluttered with toys would not have produced the Beethoven we know. His father's harsh discipline helped make him a great musician.

"My music brings me friends and regard," he wrote to his brother Johann. "What more do I want?"

Beethoven wanted much more than friends and regard or even a comfortable living. The great ferment of musical creation stirring in his mind would not let him rest. To further his basic understanding of composition, he continued to take lessons from "Papa" Haydn even though the two musicians did not see eye to eye on the subject.

Beethoven improvising on the piano for the nobility of Vienna.
(Oesterreichische Nationalbibliothek, Vienna)

Beethoven had composed three trios and had played them for the first time at a soiree in Prince Lichnowsky's salon. They were well received by most of the listeners, including the prince, the Russian ambassador Count Andreas Rasumovsky, and Baron Nikolaus Zmeskall. They looked forward to obtaining copies of the trios when they were published.

Haydn was not too enthusiastic over the compositions of his pupil. They were too modern, he thought, too changed from the accepted forms of musical composition. Although they sounded better than he had expected them to, Haydn recommended that the last of the three trios not be published.

"Why not? That is the best one of all," Beethoven challenged.

"You may think so," Haydn countered, "but I am not so sure."

When they were published, the three trios for pianoforte, violin, and cello appeared as Opus 1 and were well liked—particularly the third, in C Minor. (*Opus* means "work." A musician's compositions are usually numbered Opus 1, Opus 2, etc., to indicate the chronological order in which they appeared.) When asked about his earlier opinion of the trios, Haydn answered that he "had not believed that this trio would be so quickly and easily understood and so favorably received by the public."

The difference in opinion caused a rift between Beethoven and Haydn. The young innovator thought that his teacher was envious of him and might delay his acceptance as a composer.

The trios, although designated as Opus 1, were not Beethoven's first work. He had composed some variations, which he dedicated to Eleonore von Breuning. He sent them to Bonn with a letter of apology for not having written in almost a year. Before leaving for Vienna, he had created an unpleasant scene at the von Breuning home when Eleonore's engagement to Franz Wegeler was announced. His Lorchen had disappointed him. It was the first of many occasions when his bad temper would be unleashed, to his later embarrassment and anguish.

Haydn was not too pleased that Beethoven had dedicated his trios to Prince Lichnowsky instead of to his music teacher; he suggested that the composer write "Pupil of Haydn" on the title page. This roused Beethoven's ire, because he considered Haydn too engrossed in his own works to bother much with him. Fortunately, Haydn was leaving for a concert tour of England and was only too glad to turn his headstrong pupil over to other music teachers.

Johann Schenk, a teacher and composer of excellent reputation, chanced to see one of Beethoven's early lesson sheets. He was surprised to find that Haydn had not bothered to correct the many obvious errors in counterpoint. Schenk agreed to give Beethoven lessons without any fee and in secrecy. If Haydn was too preoccupied with his own works, Schenk was not. Beethoven's secret teacher filled in the basic gaps in his knowledge of composition. As every great artist must do, Beethoven had to undergo a period of discipline and training before he could follow his musical inspiration.

By the spring of 1794, Beethoven had begun his studies in composition with Johann Georg Albrechtsberger and Antonio Salieri. They taught him the hard-and-fast rules of counterpoint, called musical skeletons by Beethoven. There is no doubt that he was irritated by the strict disciplines of his conservative teachers. He did not enjoy the many months of boring study or the blind obedience to musical rules that had been obeyed without challenge for so many decades.

"No, Beethoven never learned anything," Albrechtsberger later remarked with a resigned shake of his head, "and what's more, he never *will* write anything worthwhile."

In spite of himself, Beethoven acquired the disciplines and theory of musical composition, but he learned many of the rules only to find effective ways of breaking them. The new spirit of freedom, independence, and liberty that was sweeping over Europe at that time was in key with Beethoven's rebellion. Blind adherence to the past was for the guidance of pygmies in the art of music, not for him.

"The rules forbid this succession of chords. Very well, I allow it," he once remarked.

As a result of his independence, Beethoven introduced an element of surprise into his music—a more complete expression of the art and a break from the limits of the past. He continued to violate the accepted rules of music. When he wrote a bold and daring innovation in form or harmony, he would make a notation in the margin for Haydn: "Is that permitted?"

An Englishwoman once overheard a conversation in a Viennese salon where Haydn was talking to his pupil Beethoven.

"You will accomplish more than has yet been accomplished—have thoughts that no other has had. You will never sacrifice a beautiful idea to a tyrannical rule, and in that you will be right. But you will sacrifice rules to your moods, for you seem to be a man of many heads and many hearts.

"One will always find something irregular in your compositions—something of beauty, but rather dark and strange, because you too are rather obscure and strange. In my works you will more often find something jovial, because that is what I am. Nothing could shake my natural cheerfulness, not even my wife."

As independent as he was in music, Beethoven was equally so in his living habits. He was getting along very well in Vienna and living a life completely free of want or privation. Generous Prince Lichnowsky was his chief patron and took him into his palatial home as a nonpaying permanent guest. Prince Karl enjoyed Beethoven's music and felt that he was helping art by nurturing the budding genius of his moody though brilliant guest. Franz Wegeler has passed along some enlightening notes on Beethoven's life when they both lived in Vienna.

Karl, Prince Lichnowsky, was a very great patron—a friend of Beethoven's, who took him into his house as a guest, where he remained a few years. I found him there toward the end of the year 1794 and he was still there in the middle of 1796. Meanwhile, Beethoven almost always rented a home in the country.

The prince was a great lover of music and a connoisseur of it. He played the pianoforte and studied Beethoven's compositions, playing them more or less well. He sought to convince Beethoven that there was no need of changing anything in his style, though he often called the composer's attention to the difficulties of his works.

There were performances at his house every Friday morning, participated in by four hired musicians—Schuppanzigh, Weiss, Kraft, and one other. Also generally attending was an amateur, Zmeskall. Here the new compositions of Beethoven, so far as was feasible, were first performed. There were usually present several great musicians and music lovers.

Beethoven frequently amazed his friends with his remarkable musicianship. Wegeler recalled several stories relating to this.

A Hungarian count once placed a difficult composition by Bach in manuscript form before Beethoven, which he played at first sight exactly as Bach would have played it.

The Viennese author Förster once brought Beethoven a quartet of which he had made a clean copy only that morning. In the second portion of the first movement the violoncello lost his place. Beethoven stood up, and still playing his own part, sang the bass accompaniment. When I spoke about it to him as proof of extraordinary accomplishment, he replied with a smile: "The bass part had to be so, else the author would have known nothing about composition."

To the remark that he had played a *presto* which he had never seen before so rapidly that it must have been impossible to see the individual notes, he answered: "Nor is that necessary. If you read rapidly, there may be a multitude of typographical errors, but you neither see nor give heed to them so long as the language is a familiar one."

At Vienna's Burgtheater, in 1795, when he was only twenty-four years old, Beethoven had his first opportunity to play before a large audience. Two concerts were given for the benefit of the widows and orphans of members of the Society of Musicians. On the program was the premiere of Concerto No. 2 for Piano and Orchestra. It was played by the promising young composer Ludwig van Beethoven.

The program was arranged by Salieri, one of Beethoven's teachers, who took this opportunity to feature his brilliant pupil. The next evening Beethoven played a Mozart concerto at a concert given for the benefit of Mozart's widow.

Beethoven remained unchallenged as the greatest pianist in Vienna until eighteen-year-old Joseph Wölffl of Salzburg arrived. He contested Beethoven's supremacy on the piano with his brilliant technique. He played with amazing ease. Beethoven was sometimes criticized for his rough and indistinct playing, although he was never surpassed in his infinite variety of improvisations.

The brilliant conductor and composer Ignaz von Seyfried described the artistry of the two great pianists.

Beethoven had already attracted attention to himself by several compositions and was rated a first-class pianist in Vienna when he was confronted by a rival in the closing years of the last [eighteenth] century. At the head of Beethoven's admirers stood the amiable Prince Lichnowsky. Among the most zealous patrons of Wölffl was the broadly cultured Baron Raymond von Wetzlar, whose delightful villa offered to all artists, native and foreign, an asylum in the summer months.

There the interesting combats of the two "gladiators" not infrequently offered an indescribable artistic treat to the numerous and thoroughly select gathering. Each brought forward the latest product of his mind. Now one and then the other gave free rein to his glowing fancy. Sometimes they would seat themselves at two pianofortes and improvise alternately on themes which they gave each other, and thus create many a four-hand capriccio which, if it could have been put upon paper, would surely have stood the test of time.

It would have been difficult, perhaps impossible, to award the palm of victory to either one of the gladiators in respect to technical skill. Nature had been kind to Wölffl in bestowing upon him a gigantic hand which could span a tenth·as easily as other hands compass an octave. It permitted him to play passages of double notes in these intervals with the rapidity of lightning.

In his improvisations even then, Beethoven did not deny his tendency toward the mysterious and gloomy. When he began to revel in the infinite world of tones, he was transported also above all earthly things. His spirit had burst all restricting bonds, shaken off the yoke of servitude, and soared triumphantly and jubilantly into the luminous spaces. Now his playing tore along like a wildly foaming cataract, and the conjurer constrained his instrument to an utterance so forceful that the stoutest structure was scarcely able to withstand it. Then he sank down, exhausted, exhaling gentle plaints, dissolving in melancholy. Again the spirit would soar aloft, triumphing over transitory terrestrial sufferings, turn its glance upward in reverent sounds, and find rest and comfort on the innocent bosom of holy nature.

Wölffl, on the contrary, trained in the school of Mozart, was always equable—never superficial, but always clear and thus more accessible to the multitude. They respected each other because they knew best how to appreciate each other. As straightforward, honest Germans, they followed the principle that the roadway of art is broad enough for many, and that it is not necessary to lose one's self in envy while pushing forward for the goal of fame.

Beethoven continued to give many concerts to the elite of Vienna. As his skill in creating original music developed he played more and more of his own compositions. In December, 1795, an advertisement in the newspaper *Die Wiener Zeitung* read, "In the Redoutensaal, Herr van Beethoven will play a concerto of his composing on the pianoforte, and three grand symphonies which the *Kapellmeister* [Haydn] composed during his last sojourn in London."

Beethoven often amazed his audience with his feats on the piano. He first played his Concerto in B-flat on a piano inadvertently tuned a half note lower than the orchestra. Unperturbed, Beethoven immediately transposed the concerto into the key of B. As any pianist knows, it is not easy to ripple over the keys faultlessly in five sharps at a moment's notice, when the music is written in two flats. His excellent training with Neefe in Bonn while learning to play Bach's *Well-tempered Clavier* again proved advantageous.

Another of Beethoven's musical feats occurred when a pianist named Daniel Steibelt showed off his flashy technique by playing on a theme from one of Beethoven's trios.

"This incensed Beethoven and his admirers," Ries wrote. "He had to go to the pianoforte and improvise. He went in his usual brusque manner to the instrument, as if half pushed, grabbing the violoncello part of Steibelt's quintet as he passed. He placed it upon the stand upside down, and with one finger drummed a theme out of the first few measures. Insulted and angered, he improvised in such a manner that Steibelt left the room before he had finished. He would never again meet Beethoven, and before he would accept any invitation, made it a condition that Beethoven should not be invited."

Beethoven had come far since he first arrived in Vienna, but true greatness was still ahead. Beethoven the pianist and improviser had opened the door for Beethoven the composer.

FOUR

"There Is Only One Beethoven"

"Courage! Despite all the weaknesses of the body, my spirit shall rule! Here I am twenty-five years old. This year must bring out the complete man." One can almost see Beethoven's determined expression as he scribbled these words in the margin of his sketchbook with his crude carpenter's pencil in the year 1796.

The words could have been written by Napoleon, Caesar, Alexander the Great, or any other young man determined to conquer the world. Beethoven was determined to conquer the world of music.

He was still living at Prince Lichnowsky's palatial home and his spirit of independence now and then got out of hand. Often he was rude and gruff to his patrons and his best friends. Haydn referred to him with amusement as the Great Mogul.

Beethoven's sense of humor was usually at the expense of others; he could not tolerate having fun poked at himself. Ignaz Schuppanzigh, a fine violinist of ample proportions, was nicknamed M'Lord Falstaff by Beethoven. Baron Nikolaus Zmeskall von Domanovecz was a skilled cellist who provided Beethoven with quill pens in return for various good-natured insults such as: "My dearest Baron Muckcart-driver, I forbid you henceforth to rob me of the good humor into which I occasionally fall, for yesterday your Zmeskall-Domanoveczian chatter made me melancholy. The devil take you. I want none of your moral principles."

Again, Beethoven wrote to the same genial nobleman as only one friend could write to another.

Best of Music Counts!

I beg of you to send me one or a few pens, of which I am really in great need. As soon as I learn where really good and admirable pens are to be found, I will buy some of them. I hope to see you at the Swan today. Adieu, most precious Music Count.

While Beethoven's fame as a composer gathered momentum in the favorable atmosphere of Vienna his ties with Bonn were gradually vanishing. His brother Karl made his home in Vienna in 1794, and Johann arrived the next year. Karl received help from his brother in establishing himself as a musician and music teacher; the name Beethoven now opened many doors in Vienna. Unfortunately, Karl took undue advantage of his brother's fame and often embarrassed him.

Johann had finished his apprenticeship as a druggist and worked in an apothecary shop on the Kärnthnerstrasse. Over the shop hung a sign with the interesting name, *Zum Heiligen Geist* (To the Holy Ghost).

Beethoven left Vienna on a concert tour with Prince Lichnowsky in February, 1796. He wrote a letter from Prague to his brother Johann, "to be delivered at the apothecary shop near the Kärnthner Gate."

> I shall remain here a few weeks more and then go to Dresden, Leipzig, and Berlin. It will probably be six more weeks before I return. I hope that you will be increasingly pleased with your sojourn in Vienna, but beware of the whole group of wicked women.
>
> Prince Lichnowsky will probably soon return to Vienna. If you need money, you may go to him boldly, for he still owes me some. For the rest, I hope that your life will grow continually in happiness and to that end I hope to contribute something.
>
> Farewell, dear brother, and think occasionally of
>
> Your true, faithful brother, L. Beethoven.

During his travels, Beethoven visited Dresden, where he played for the Elector of Saxony for an hour and a half. His Royal Highness chose to share Beethoven's

E

playing with no one as he sat alone enjoying the music. In Berlin, Beethoven played at the court of Friedrich Wilhelm II, and so delighted the king that he presented Beethoven with a gold snuffbox filled with gold louis. According to Beethoven, "It was not an ordinary snuffbox, but such a one as might have been given to an ambassador."

The king, a nephew of Frederick the Great, was a dedicated lover of music. He played the cello—or violoncello—in quartets and at rehearsals for the opera performances. Good music was so much a part of high society in those days that a well-educated and cultured nobleman would not consider his education complete without learning some musical skill or gaining some knowledge of music.

During his visit to Berlin, Beethoven became acquainted with the pianist Friedrich Heinrich Himmel. He judged Himmel's playing as a "pretty talent, but no more. His pianoforte playing was elegant and pleasing, but he was not to be compared with Prince Louis Ferdinand."

After Beethoven returned to Vienna he spent much of his time playing concerts in the great houses of the city, and continued his studies in composition and teaching. Many of his pupils were charming young ladies of wealth and position. There can be no doubt that he enjoyed spending an hour or two with each of them. Young and impressionable, they were equally charmed to have the famous Beethoven as a teacher. How many love affairs bloomed from the music lessons will never be known.

"There was never a time," wrote Beethoven's friend of many years, Franz Wegeler, "when Beethoven was not in love, and that in the highest degree. He occasionally made a conquest that would have been difficult, if not impossible, for many an Adonis."

"When we passed a somewhat charming girl," Ries recalled, "he would turn back and gaze keenly at her through his glasses. If he noticed that I observed him, he would laugh or grin. He was frequently in love, but only for a short period. Once when I twitted him about a pretty woman, he admitted that she had held him in the strongest bonds for the longest time—fully seven months."

Beethoven was not a handsome man, with his short, stocky body and disheveled hair. Yet many of his feminine admirers seemed to see only the best in him. His perfect teeth made his smile captivating. One young woman described his eyes as "beautiful, speaking eyes that mirror the changing expression of the moment—by turns gracious, agreeable, wild, angry, menacing."

The Countess Charlotte von Brunswick described a friend whose "physiognomy is just like Beethoven's. He has the same expressive and lively glance. You can see the genius in his eyes."

Some of the infatuations with his pretty young pupils

grew into serious love affairs. Woe betide any one of these lovely charmers, however, if they grew careless over Beethoven's only lasting love, music.

Among his young music pupils, Beethoven taught the daughters of Countess Therese von Brunswick. One day he arrived early at the door of the Brunswick home to give a lesson. He paused to listen as young Tesi practiced one of his sonatas. Although she played the notes correctly, she ignored the dynamics of the composition. Beethoven could easily forgive mistakes such as hitting a wrong note, but he could not forgive ignoring the spirit and feeling of the music.

The lesson began. Tesi had not learned the sonata by heart, and played with her eyes glued to the notes on the music sheet. She continued to play without capturing the spirit of the music. Unable to control his temper, Beethoven tore the music in two, grabbed his hat and coat, and left in anger.

When it was well played, music brought uncontrolled joy to the composer. In the last year of the eighteenth century, Domenico Dragonetti, the great bass viol player, visited Beethoven. With his usual touch of mischief when confronted by a great instrumentalist, Beethoven thought he might try to trip up Europe's best bassist. He placed his Sonata in G Minor for the Cello in front of Dragonetti, while he played the accompaniment on the piano.

With his big bass viol, Dragonetti showed his great

skill and musicianship. He continued to play the fast cello part right through the difficult arpeggio in the Rondo. Beethoven was overjoyed. Leaping up from the piano, he threw a bear hug around Dragonetti and his cumbersome instrument.

Beethoven strongly disdained the inability of many musicians to play some of the difficult parts he wrote in moments of inspired creativity. His joy at virtuosity was matched by his contempt for a musician's limitations, particularly when the musician complained that one of Beethoven's works was too difficult to play or sing.

Later, when Beethoven wrote his fast-moving passages for the bass viols in the Scherzo of his Fifth Symphony, he must have thought of Dragonetti. One can almost see the twinkle in his eyes and the demoniac smile lighting up his face as he thought of the bass players trying to play the difficult passages.

Beethoven often roared with laughter at the musical chaos caused when the musicians fell into traps of his setting. A friend described Beethoven's reaction while rehearsing his music with an orchestra.

"When playing at first sight, there were frequent pauses for the purpose of correcting the parts, and then the thread would be broken. Even then, he would be patient. When things went to pieces, particularly in the scherzos of his symphonies at a sudden and unexpected change of rhythm, he would shout with laughter. He admitted he had expected nothing else, and had reckoned on it from the beginning. He was almost childishly glad that he had been successful in unhorsing such excellent riders."

A long, intimate association with violin, viola, and cello music had given Beethoven a solid background for writing his masterful quartets for these instruments. Beethoven's friend Ignaz Schuppanzigh was a brilliant violinist and was described in *Die Allgemeine Musikalische Zeitung*, a musical periodical, as knowing how to "bring out all the fire and strength, the refinement, tenderness, humor, love, and caprice so expressively that the first violin could hardly be entrusted to better hands."

Count Rasumovsky, the Russian ambassador, retained a string quartet in his household. Schuppanzigh wrote that "Beethoven was as much at home in the Rasumovsky establishment as a hen in the coop. Everything he wrote was taken warm from the nest and tried out in the frying pan. Every note was played precisely as he wanted it played, with such devotion, love, obedience, and piety as could be inspired only by a passionate admiration of his great genius.

"It was precisely the delving into the most secret depths of the music, the total comprehension of the spirit of the work, that enabled this quartet to gain, through the playing of Beethoven's music, its universal fame. One voice alone, Beethoven's, spoke through the music and its interpretation."

No one had to acquaint Beethoven with the limitations of the piano, because he stood at the top of Viennese

Young Beethoven directs Count Rasumovsky's quartet. (British Museum, London)

piano virtuosi. He learned how to write more effectively for the French horn from Nicolaus Simrock and Johann Wenzel Stich; for the clarinet from Joseph Friedlowsky; and for the flute from Carl Scholl. There is little doubt that acquaintance with these excellent musicians helped Beethoven compose for their instruments with greater understanding. The orchestration for his symphonies and overtures certainly benefited from help given by his stimulating patrons and talented friends.

Baron Gottfried von Swieten, director of the Imperial Library, befriended the young musician and frequently invited him to his house. A friend of Mozart and Haydn, von Swieten wrote that he was "oppressed by the new evidence of decadence of the arts. My principal comforters at such times are Handel and the Bachs and those few great men of our own day who, taking these as their masters, follow resolutely in the same quest for greatness and truth."

Evidently he saw in Beethoven the "same quest for greatness and truth" that he had learned to cherish in the older masters. Mozart was dead, Haydn was growing old, and Beethoven was one of the few young men who could carry the torch of greatness into the future.

Beethoven was to have the honor of taking the torch from "Papa" Haydn, still the dean of musicians and composers in Vienna. Despite their shared interest in music, theirs had not been a fortunate teacher-pupil relationship. Haydn, then the *Kapellmeister* for Prince Esterhazy, was a busy composer in the twilight of a distinguished career. He looked back at the eighteenth century, while young Beethoven looked ahead to the nineteenth century and beyond.

Haydn, with his portly, venerable dignity, wore lacy ruffles at his neck and wrists. His white wig, curled on each side, gave him a formal, pompous appearance. In contrast, Beethoven dressed as plainly as the customs of the day permitted.

While still in Bonn, Beethoven had had opportunities to make friends with aristocratic people on terms of perfect equality through the members of the von Breuning family and Count Waldstein. This background made it easier for him to mingle with the titled people he met in Vienna. Prince Karl Lichnowsky and his brother, Count Moritz, had studied under Mozart. Both of them were talented pianists. Karl's wife, Princess Maria Christiane, was also well educated and a great music enthusiast. "The princess would like to have enclosed me in a glass bell," Beethoven commented, "so that the unworthy might neither touch nor breathe upon me."

Baroness Dorothea von Ertmann was a magnificent pianist; Prince Franz Josef von Lobkovitz played the violin well; and Count Franz von Brunswick played with confidence on the cello. Prince Nikolaus Esterhazy played a cellolike instrument called a baritone, while his brother, Count Franz Esterhazy, played the oboe. In this royal realm of music, Beethoven considered himself at least their equal, if not king of them all.

Among Beethoven's friends in Vienna there were

many who were not of royal blood and high position. These companions were members of the musical fraternity, who lived by the patronage of the aristocracy. One of Beethoven's closest friends, Karl Amenda, was a theological student and an excellent violinist. He worked for Prince Lobkovitz for a while, and was a music teacher to Frau Mozart's family.

Amenda had hoped that someday he might meet the great Beethoven. One evening while Amenda was playing first violin in a quartet, someone reached over and turned the pages during the performance. At the finish he turned around to thank his helper. What a surprise! It was Beethoven himself, nodding approval as he departed. The next day, Amenda was surprised again to hear that Beethoven requested the pleasure of his company.

Music had brought these two young men together, and the new friends played for hours on the violin and piano. At times, Amenda sat silently, entranced as he listened to Beethoven improvising on the piano.

"It is a great pity that such glorious music is born and lost in a moment," he remarked.

"There you are mistaken," replied Beethoven. "I can repeat every extemporization."

To prove it, he sat down at the keyboard and played the same music as before without a change. Unfortunately, Beethoven did not pick up his quill pen to write down the notes, and we do not know how much of this music lived beyond the composer's lifetime.

Beethoven permitted his titled friends to patronize and assist him although he would never permit them to dictate to him. His only master was the art of music, which he served without stint or compromise.

Even his pupil Archduke Rudolph was given a sharp twist of the fingers for keeping Beethoven waiting a few minutes. Surprised, the archduke inquired why his teacher was so impatient.

"You wasted my time in the waiting room," Beethoven growled.

Nevertheless, Beethoven's letters are full of excuses to Rudolph for not appearing at all for scheduled lessons.

One day in Baden, Beethoven and Ries were playing piano and violin in Count von Browne's salon. The magic spell of the music was suddenly shattered by the loud voice of Count Palffy in the next room. This was intolerable! Beethoven quickly sprang up from his piano seat and announced in a loud voice, "For such swine I do not play." His quick and violent temper was often coupled with a harsh rudeness that a polished gentleman would not have permitted himself.

Beethoven was sensitive about being called upon to perform at any time. The servile place of music and musicians in those days might have been acceptable to others, but not to Beethoven. This was a new era when liberty and equality were asserting themselves. Was not the French Revolution already over? Was not the low-born General Bonaparte running over the sovereignties of

Europe with one victory after another? In this atmosphere, Beethoven's spunky attitude flourished; he despised the old order of servility.

He would not play for his dinner, nor at the convenience of the pampered members of society who took him in as their own. Princess Maria Christiane Lichnowsky could plead in vain for him to improvise for her guests on the piano. It would have made no difference if a king or a queen had made the request; he steadfastly refused to play when he did not feel like it.

At times he went too far in his disdain for the titled noblemen. His carefree existence at the Lichnowsky mansion was doomed to end, for Beethoven quarreled with the prince and had to find other quarters. When he left the Lichnowsky house he smashed the plaster bust of his good friend and generous patron. He hurried out of the palatial home and slammed the door. Later he wrote a note:

> Prince, what you are, you are by accident of birth. What I am, I am of myself. There are and will be thousands of princes. There is only one Beethoven.

Without Lichnowsky's patronage, Beethoven's cost of living rose, and he managed his money badly. At the same time, his generosity to his friends continued without regard for the rent coming due or bills piling up.

One day he mentioned to Karl Amenda that he was

often embarrassed for want of money and had no idea how to pay his overdue rent.

"That's easily remedied," Amenda replied lightly.

He gave Beethoven a theme on which to write variations and locked him in his room. He would be back in three hours to see how he was progressing. When Amenda returned, Beethoven handed him the completed variations, entitled *Freudvoll und Leidvoll* (*Joyful and Sorrowful*), with the ill-tempered remark, "Here is the rag!"

Amenda gave the composition to the landlord with instructions to take it to a music publisher, who would reward him well. Returning in glee, the landlord asked if Beethoven had any more such bits of paper around.

Beethoven found the tiresome money shortages irksome, and Amenda suggested a tour of Italy to free him from his financial problems. He agreed to go with Beethoven, and plans were already afoot when bad news intervened. Amenda's brother had been killed in an accident and he had to return to his home in Courland to assume family responsibilities. Upon parting from his good friend, Beethoven gave Amenda a copy of his Quartet in F Major, Opus 18. On the first violin part he had written:

Dear Amenda:

Take this quartet as a small memorial of our friendship, and whenever you play it recall the days which we passed together and the sincere affection felt for you then and which will always be felt by.

> Your warm and true friend,
> Ludwig van Beethoven

While he had good friends in Vienna, Beethoven also had many enemies in the musical community. Some of the local musicians resented the invasion of a musician from another country, and Beethoven's success created numerous professional jealousies. He was a perfect target, for his poor manners and his idiosyncrasies provided plenty of grist for the gossip mills. Some of the music critics made caustic remarks about his music, for it was too radical and innovative for their taste.

Beethoven followed the beckoning of his star. He scorned those who did not understand his compositions, yet he often felt persecuted because those of small stature in the art of music tried to belittle him through their cynical gossip and slander. The giant remained a giant, though at times a bitter one.

"Let them talk," he remarked. "Their chatter will certainly never render anyone immortal, any more than it can take away the immortality of a person whom Apollo has chosen."

The success of Napoleon's first Italian campaign directly affected Beethoven's life. The French Directory had followed the victories of the French armies with costly demands after the peace of Campo Formio. General Jean Baptiste Bernadotte was appointed as the new Minister to hold jurisdiction over all Frenchmen in the Austrian Empire. He arrived in Vienna in February, 1798.

Young General Bonaparte had set all Europe talking, and Bernadotte suggested to Beethoven that he write a symphony expressing the heroic spirit of the great military leader. At this time, Beethoven had strong republican leanings and admired the daring exploits of the bold French general who he thought was advancing the cause of liberty, equality, and fraternity. The inspiration for a dynamic symphony was born. Later it emerged as his Third Symphony, the *Eroica*.

FIVE

"*I Am Resolved To Rise Above Every Obstacle*"

The year 1800 marked not only the end of the eighteenth century but also the beginning of a new world more attuned to the spirit of Beethoven. He was spending more time at his desk, quill pen in hand, composing. He had written numerous sonatas, trios, variations, songs, and miscellaneous compositions. Among them was the quartet he had given to Karl Amenda as a parting gift.

Beethoven realized that he had not mastered the technique of quartet writing and sent a message to his friend.

Do not lend your quartet to anybody. I have greatly changed it, having just learned how to write quartets properly, as you will observe when you receive them.

F

In the same letter, Beethoven, the foremost pianist of Vienna, wrote that he had greatly improved his pianoforte playing and planned to make a tour as a virtuoso. The tour was never to be made. Fate stepped in and, like the distant rumbling of thunder, announced a great storm in Beethoven's life. The genius of the keyboard and of composition, the entrancer of the music salons of Vienna, was growing deaf. He wrote again to his friend Karl:

Your Beethoven is living an unhappy life, quarreling with nature and its Creator, often cursing the latter for surrendering his creatures to the merest accident which often breaks or destroys the most beautiful blossoms. Know that my noblest faculty, *my hearing*, has greatly deteriorated. The most beautiful years of my life must pass by without my accomplishing all that my talent and powers bid me to do. A sad resignation must be my refuge, although indeed, I am resolved to rise above every obstacle.

That is the spirit of Beethoven. He would not give in easily. Still, he had wanted no one to know of his malady, for he hoped that he might overcome his deafness.

"I beg of you to keep the matter of my deafness a profound secret," he implored Amenda, "to be confided to nobody, no matter whom."

Later, Beethoven poured out his heart to his friend Franz Wegeler.

I can truly say that I am living a wretched life. For two years I have avoided almost all social gatherings because it is impossible for me to say to people, "I am deaf." If I belonged to any other profession it would be easier, but in my profession it is a frightful state. Then there are my enemies, who are numerous. What would they say about this?

In the theater I must get very close to the orchestra in order to understand the actor, and if I am a little distant I do not hear the high tones of the instruments or singers. It is curious that in conversation there are people who do not notice my condition at all. Since I have generally been absent-minded, they account for it in that way. Often I can scarcely hear someone speaking softly—the tones, yes, but not the words. However, as soon as anyone shouts, it is intolerable.

Heaven knows what will happen to me! But Plutarch has taught me resignation. If possible, I will bid defiance to my fate, although there will be moments in my life when I shall be the unhappiest of God's creatures.

The gathering storm inside Beethoven was a secret that he confided only to his two friends Karl Amenda and

Franz Wegeler, to whom he could write freely. Beethoven had hoped to play the piano on tours, compose music, and lead a full and happy life among his friends. This was not to be.

Beethoven's creative powers would be directed more and more toward composing, and increasingly less toward performing as a musician. His listeners in the music salons of Europe suffered a great loss. But the world reaped a rich harvest of music that would continue to live centuries after Beethoven's aristocratic audiences had left their candlelit concert salons.

By the time Beethoven had reached the age of thirty, he had "composed everything except opera and church music." His First Symphony was presented at a public concert on April 2, 1800, at the Royal Imperial Court Theater.

Why had he waited so long to write "a new grand symphony with complete orchestra"?

Vienna had no permanent symphony orchestra in those days. At that time, a complete orchestra had to be made up of local musicians assembled for the occasion. Because there was no permanently established orchestra, the demand was not as great for Beethoven to write symphonies as it was for him to compose trios, sonatas, concertos, and variations to be played by small groups in the great houses of Vienna.

Unlike Mozart, Beethoven had developed slowly as a composer. He wrote for a full orchestra only after he had served an apprenticeship in writing for small ensembles and after he had learned to compose effectively for the various groups of instruments: strings, brass, woodwinds, and percussion.

It was fitting for this composer of the new century to unveil his First Symphony in the year 1800. The opening chord of the symphony, a dominant seventh, sounded harsh and wrong to the critics. Following that opening chord, the music took on the flavor and form of the past century—the rococo embellishments of Mozart and Haydn.

This was Beethoven's first attempt at composing a symphony, and his work compared favorably with any other then known. That first chord was only a promise, which would be honored at a later date.

On the same program that introduced Beethoven's First Symphony were a symphony by Mozart; two selections from *The Creation*, an oratorio by Haydn; a piano concerto composed and played by Beethoven; and a septet for four string and three wind instruments, dedicated by Beethoven to the Empress Maria Theresa. One program number featured Beethoven improvising on the piano.

The orchestra refused to respond to the conductor's baton, and Beethoven's First Symphony was given a very shoddy introduction to the world. His septet, however, with Schuppanzigh leading in the first violin part, was launched into immediate popularity. Beethoven the pianist was emerging into Beethoven the composer.

During the summer months, Beethoven looked forward to his visits in the country. He usually found lodging in some little town such as Unterdöbling, where he could wander across the fields, through the woods, or along a rippling stream. Here his thoughts were free of society's trivia. Here was a place where he could attune his mind and his inspiration to nature. No one loved the great outdoors better than this eccentric composer. Later he captured the joy of nature in his musical compositions.

As he strolled along in the country he would hum a theme and stop abruptly to jot down notes with his clumsy carpenter's pencil. At times, he would relax under a big tree and look up at the clouds drifting by. Oblivious of those who might be nearby, he would wave his arms, stamp his feet, or sing in a frightful manner. Who would guess that this short, ungainly man, stumbling along over the rough turf, scribbling with his stumpy pencil in a dog-eared notebook, was originating such heaven-sent music?

Back in Vienna, the cold, sharp winds of the winter of 1800 brought bad news. The French victory at Hohenlinden in December was a disaster for Austria. The hospitals were crowded with the wounded and the dying. Soldiers and their families were left in trying circumstances. Many of the husbands and fathers would never again be able to work on their farms or in their shops. Thousands of the men never would return.

A series of concerts was one of the means of raising

money to relieve the suffering of the grief-stricken families. Beethoven played the piano; Haydn directed his symphonies; and many of the other musical stars of Vienna performed or organized concerts for charity. While Beethoven did not become directly involved in the fighting, he was never far away from war's horrible impact.

"When you see me again," he wrote to Franz Wegeler the next June, "it will be only as a great man, not only a greater artist but a better and more accomplished man. If conditions are improved in our fatherland, my art will be used only in the service of the poor."

In the matter of finances, Beethoven's situation was "not so bad," he wrote.

In the last year, unbelievable as it may sound when I tell you, Lichnowsky, who has always remained my warmest friend (there were little quarrels between us, but haven't they served to strengthen our friendship?), has set aside a fixed sum of 600 florins for me to draw upon so long as I remain without a post suitable for me.

My compositions bring me a fair sum, and I may say that I have more commissions than it is possible for me to fill. Besides, I have six or seven publishers after each piece and might have more if I chose. People no longer bargain with me. I ask and they pay. If I see a friend in need and my purse does not permit me to help him at once, I have only to get to work, and in a short time, help is at hand.

Beethoven's kindness was rewarded. In addition to the six hundred florins, the generous prince gave him a quartet of very fine instruments: two violins, a viola, and a cello. They were then about one hundred years old. Expensive at that time, they are priceless now. The instruments can no longer be heard, but they can be seen at the Beethoven-Haus in Bonn.

Beethoven eagerly explored new forms of musical expression. His ballet music *The Creations of Prometheus*, Opus 43, was first performed in March, 1801. Haydn, who had just heard the music, chanced to meet his former pupil on the street.

"Well, I heard your ballet yesterday and it pleased me very much," the venerable composer remarked.

Beethoven was always ready for a pun. "Ah, dear Papa, you are very kind, but it is far from being a *Creation*," he quipped, referring to Haydn's oratorio of the same name.

Haydn, showing no sense of humor, replied, "That is true. It is not yet a creation, and I hardly believe that it will ever become one."

The ups and downs in Beethoven's life at this time were reflected in his letters to Wegeler and Amenda. In letters to Wegeler, the composer writes of "that evil

Stringed instruments that once belonged to Beethoven, now on display at the Beethoven-Haus. (Beethoven-Haus, Bonn)

demon, my bad health—frightful attacks of colic—ears
hum and buzz continually, day and night."

On the brighter side, he was very happy to see his old
friend Stephan von Breuning, "a good, splendid young
fellow," who had recently come to Vienna from Bonn.
Still, his bad hearing haunted him like a ghost. He wrote
to Franz Wegeler in Bonn :

> I seemed like a misanthrope, and yet am far
> from being one. This change has been wrought by
> a dear, fascinating girl who loves me and whom I
> love. There have been a few blessed moments
> within the last two years, and it is the first time
> that I feel that marriage might bring me happiness.
> Unfortunately, she is not of my station—and now
> —it would be impossible for me to marry.

The "fascinating" girl was Countess Giulietta Guic-
ciardi, daughter of an Austrian court councillor. A
beautiful young lady of sixteen (almost fourteen years
younger than Beethoven), Giulietta was dazzled by the
attentions of the famous pianist and composer.

She took piano lessons from Beethoven, and loved good
music. He gave his Rondo in G Major, Opus 51, to the
young countess, but when he needed a composition to
dedicate to Countess Henriette Lichnowsky, he asked
Giulietta to return it. To make amends, Beethoven later
dedicated his *Moonlight* Sonata to Giulietta.

There was never to be a happy ending to the love story

of Giulietta and Beethoven. Later she married Count Wenzel Robert Gallenberg. Neither of the two lovers found happiness apart, yet it seems doubtful that Giulietta would have been content with Beethoven, who spent most of his time with his music.

Six years before, Beethoven had met Magdalene Willmann, an opera singer from Bonn, who would not consider marrying the eccentric composer. After Giulietta married, his affections were captured by Countess Anna Marie Erdödy, to whom he dedicated two trios, in D Major and E-flat Major, Opus 70, and two sonatas for piano and cello, in C Major and D Major, Opus 102.

Various other lovely ladies of taste, talent, and position tugged at Beethoven's heartstrings, but love passed him by time and again. It is perhaps fortunate for posterity that it was so. His dreams of love and happiness were sublimated into his music. This music might never have been written if he had been happily married.

Rejected by love, Beethoven sought refuge in his music. This refuge was about to be taken away from him too, for his hearing was slowly enveloping him in an island of silence—a stillness that threatened to ruin his career. His hopes of touring Europe and the world as a concert pianist were fast disappearing. His deafness isolated him from his friends, separating him from the musical society he loved and threatening to still his music.

Gigantic forces struggled within Beethoven. He was torn between suicide and the humiliation of failure in the face of his enemies. Only one purpose in life made him hang onto hope : fulfillment of his art.

When he was thirty-one, Beethoven retreated to a peaceful little town called Heiligenstadt. Away from gay, bustling Vienna and in the quiet of the beautiful countryside, he hoped in vain that his sense of hearing would improve. Alone, depressed, and shattered by false hope, he poured out his heart in the famous "Heiligenstadt Testament."

Oh, my fellowmen, who consider me hostile, declare me to be obstinate or misanthropic, how unjust you are! You do not know the hidden cause that makes me seem that way to you. My heart and my mind have, since childhood, yielded to the tender touch of human kindness. The mood was always with me to accomplish great tasks. But bear in mind that for six years a disastrous affliction has befallen me, aggravated by ignorant doctors.

Deceived from year to year in the hope that I would recover, I am forced at last to accept the prospect of a malady that may take years to heal or may prove incurable. Endowed from birth with a lively, ardent disposition, susceptible to the pleasures of human society, I was soon compelled to isolate myself and live a life of loneliness. When sometimes I overcame my fears, oh, how brutally was I repelled by the doubly agonizing realization of my bad hearing! Yet I still could not bring

One of Beethoven's retreats in Heiligenstadt, now a café.

myself to the point of saying to people, "Speak louder—shout—for I am deaf!"

How could I possibly admit a defect in the *one sense* which with me should have been more perfect than with others—a sense which I once possessed to a degree of perfection equaled only by a few in my profession now or at any time? Oh, no, I cannot do that! Therefore, forgive me whenever you see me evading you—I, who would so ardently be among you.

My misfortune hurts twofold, for it is bound to cause me to be misunderstood. For me, relaxation in human society, subtle discourse, and mutual revelation cannot exist. Almost entirely alone with myself, I may mix with my fellow creatures only when utmost necessity demands it. I must live in exile. If I approach a group of people, I am gripped by a hot wave of panic because of the risk I take of making my condition known to them.

During these six months spent in the country it was just the same. My discerning doctor met my inclinations almost halfway by advising me to spare my hearing as much as possible, though I was on occasion led astray by my yearning for human companionship.

What humiliation did I suffer if someone stood next to me and heard a flute sounding from afar and I heard nothing, or someone heard a shepherd singing—and again I heard nothing. Such happenings brought me to the brink of despair. Little more was needed for me to have ended my life; it was only my art that held me back.

It seemed impossible for me to depart this world before I had brought forth all that I felt inspired to create. So I went on living this miserable life— truly miserable—and so nervous that any sudden change could fling me from a state of well-being into the blackest gloom. Patience, they say, is what I must take for my guide. I have certainly done so. I hope my determination will remain firm until fate chooses to sever the thread of life.

Maybe things will improve, maybe not. I am composed. Forced into the role of philosopher, it is no easy matter for the artist—more difficult than for anybody else.

Oh, mankind! When one day you read this you will know that you have wronged me. The unhappy one among you can reap consolation from the fact that there was one like him who despite all the obstacles of nature went on doing all in his power to find acceptance within the ranks of celebrated artists.

In the testament, Beethoven left his "small fortune" to be "divided honestly" between his brothers.

My wish is that your lives should be happier, less worry-burdened than mine was. Impress virtue upon your children. This alone and not money can bring happiness, and I say this from experience. Virtue it was that kept me upright even in adversity. To virtue as well as to my art am I grateful for the fact that I did not end my life by suicide. Farewell, and love one another!

I should like Prince Lichnowsky's instruments to remain in the keeping of one of you, but there must be no quarrel between you about this! Should they, however, help you toward something more useful to you, do not hesitate to sell them.

Beethoven also wrote that

should death come before I have been able to develop all my creative powers, then it will have come too soon despite my hard lot. Even so, I would be content, for would it not release me from a state of never-ending suffering?

His long testament was written on October 6, 1802, and on the tenth he added:

Thus I take leave of you, and sadly so. Yes, the cherished hope I brought here with me, the hope of being cured to some extent, must now be completely abandoned. As the autumn leaves float down and fade away, so my hope has withered. I leave here almost the same as when I arrived. Even

Beethoven makes musical notations in his sketchbook as he walks in the village of Heiligenstadt. (Wiener Beethoven-Gesellschaft, Heiligenstadt)

Statue of Beethoven in Heiligenstadt.

the lofty courage that inspired me during the beautiful summer days has disappeared.

Oh, Providence! Permit me once again to experience a day of pure happiness! For so long now, the inner echo of true joy has remained unknown to me. When, oh God, in the temple of nature and of mankind can I again find it? Never? Oh, no, that would be too cruel to bear!"

This was Beethoven's letter of resignation to his fate of deafness. Although he could hardly hear, he went on to compose inspired works. His greatest music was yet to be written.

SIX

"What I Have in My Heart Must Out"

The "Heiligenstadt Testament" marked a low point in Beethoven's spirits, but it also marked a point of departure, a springboard to greater creativity. His friends knew nothing of the composer's testament. It was discovered among his papers after his death.

The year 1803 was the beginning of a highly productive period in Beethoven's life. The first performance of his oratorio *Christ on the Mount of Olives*, Opus 85, was given on April 8. Some parts of this oratorio were written and arranged in haste. On the morning of the final rehearsal, Ferdinand Ries called on Beethoven and found him still in bed, writing on separate sheets of paper. When Ries asked what he was writing, Beethoven answered, "Trombones."

With their music added as an afterthought, the confused trombone players tried to follow their parts from the composer's hastily scribbled sheets. It is little wonder that the rehearsal that started at eight in the morning went so badly.

"It was a terrible rehearsal," Ries recalled. "At half-past two everybody was exhausted and dissatisfied. Prince Karl Lichnowsky, who had attended the rehearsal from the beginning, sent for bread and butter, cold meat, and wine in large baskets. He pleasantly asked all to help themselves. This they did with both hands, and good nature was restored again."

The concert was a rather lengthy one, for it included Beethoven's First Symphony and his Second Symphony, his Piano Concerto in C Minor, Opus 37, and *Christ on the Mount of Olives*.

The oratorio was Beethoven's first dramatic work and was not very successful.

The Second Symphony, Opus 36, had been completed the year before, in 1802. The orchestra, a group of musicians gathered from here and there, barely managed to play the music in tune and tempo. Capturing its magic was quite beyond them. In this work, Beethoven introduced the scherzo (fast and sprightly) movement into a symphony for the first time—a notable innovation. He did not consciously try to create something new; he wrote to express his art in the way that he thought best.

"The new and original," he said, "is born of itself without one's thinking of it."

The music critics thought that Beethoven was striving too hard for originality. The Second Symphony was a bridge between the eighteenth and the nineteenth centuries. It holds an important place in the history of symphonic music, for Beethoven was boldly exploring new ground. The critics had little vision, and were sure that the composer's creative trend had landed him in quicksand.

Beethoven was not concerned with the reviews of the critics. He was much too busy working on his Third Symphony. The suggestion of General Bernadotte, made five years earlier, that he write a major composition symbolic of Napoleon's glorious victories had not been forgotten.

Beethoven was a year younger than Napoleon and they both rose to greatness, one by composing and the other by conquest. It was only natural that a man of Beethoven's republican sentiments should have great admiration for the First Consul of France—the man who had restored order out of the chaos of revolution.

With his advanced attitudes concerning liberty and equality, Beethoven did not endear himself to the Austrian emperor. He was tolerated in Vienna only because the emperor's son, Archduke Rudolph, was one of his music pupils.

France was Austria's worst enemy, and Napoleon was considered the greatest threat to peace. Humiliating defeats, thousands of Austrian soldiers dead, harsh peace terms—these were the results of France's new republic, as viewed from the emperor's palace at Schönbrunn.

From Beethoven's viewpoint, Napoleon was the heroic inspiration for a grand artistic creation, the Third Symphony. By working constantly, Beethoven finished his Third Symphony, Opus 55, in 1804. It was an overwhelming, epoch-making masterpiece written with intensity in broad, bold lines, and crashed through the barriers of past tradition, old rules, and known musical forms.

While Beethoven was writing his Third Symphony, Stephan von Breuning knocked at the door of his house to introduce Willibrord Joseph Mähler to the composer. Mähler, a cultivated gentleman, was also a skilled amateur portrait painter. When he expressed a desire to hear Beethoven play, the composer sat down at the piano and started to perform his new symphony. He continued for two hours, enchanting Mähler as he played.

"There was not a measure that was faulty or did not sound original," Mähler recalled. "Beethoven played with his hands so still—there was no tossing them to and fro, up and down. They seemed to glide to right and left over the keys, the fingers alone doing their work."

In May, 1804, the "Bonaparte" Symphony was being copied so that it might be sent to Napoleon in Paris. Later, Ries wrote:

In this symphony, Beethoven had Bonaparte in mind, as First Consul. Beethoven esteemed him greatly at the time, and likened him to the greatest Roman consuls. I, as well as several of his more intimate friends, saw a copy of the score lying upon his table, with the word "Buonaparte" at the extreme top of the title page. At the extreme bottom (also with the Italian spelling) was "Luigi van Beethoven."

I was the first to bring him the news that Bonaparte had proclaimed himself emperor. He flew into a rage and exclaimed: "So he is also nothing more than an ordinary man! Now he will trample on the rights of mankind and indulge only his own ambitions. From now on, he will make himself superior to all others and become a tyrant."

Beethoven went to the table, took hold of the title page by the top, tore it in two, and threw it on the floor. The first page was rewritten and only then did the symphony receive the title *Sinfonia Eroica*.

The symphony was not well received at its premiere performance. The music critics considered it a disjointed, grotesque musical monster. The unity and fire that Beethoven had infused into this "monster" were too much for them to grasp. The audience was not prepared for such a giant step forward in its musical fare. Their ears were still attuned to the past. At the first performance of the *Eroica* they heard the grand opening of a new era in music without even suspecting that anything great had been played.

Instead of being delivered to Paris in the diplomatic pouch with the mail from the French embassy in Vienna, the *Eroica* stayed for some time where it was written, its title page ripped in two and cast aside. Had it been delivered to Napoleon as intended, the symphony would surely have brought a handsome sum of money. By tearing it apart, Beethoven may have indulged in the most expensive gesture of his life. No one will ever know how much it cost him, but one thing is sure: regardless of the cost, Beethoven would not have had it any other way.

With the dark, depressing realization that he would have to accept a life in the silent world of increasing deafness, Beethoven lived between hope and despair. To write the glorious, powerful, and jubilant music of the *Eroica* called for a heroic effort on his part. Many of his biographers agree that only Beethoven could equal the heroic greatness portrayed in his Third Symphony.

Napoleon had ushered in a new Europe with a prelude of cannon, a theme of might makes right, and a finale of fame and glory. By audacity and conquest he had fashioned his new world from the confusion of the French Revolution. Beethoven created his new world of music by an equally bold departure from the past. In that sense they were both rebels, revolutionaries, men who were destined to change the world around them.

Napoleon flourished on renown and glory. Beethoven scorned fame for itself. When reference was made to his youthful renown, Beethoven scoffed, *"Ach, Dummheit! I have never thought of writing for fame and glory. What I have in my heart must out—that is why I write."*

Beethoven usually had several compositions on his mind at one time. When his progress on one faltered, he turned his attention to another. His great productivity during this period is reflected in his creations during 1803 and 1804. In addition to his Third Symphony, he wrote the Piano Sonata in C Major, Opus 53, the *Waldstein* Sonata, dedicated to Count Waldstein; the Concerto in C Major for Piano, Violin, Cello, and Orchestra, Opus 56, written for his piano pupil Archduke Rudolph; an Andante in F Major for piano; a Bagatelle in C Major for piano; the Piano Sonata in F Major, Opus 54; and the song *"Gedenke Mein"* ("Remember me").

The Andante in F Major for piano, originally intended to be part of the sonata dedicated to Count Waldstein, was very popular and was a great favorite of Beethoven's. For this reason he called it *Andante Favori*. His pupil Ferdinand Ries later recalled an incident concerning it.

> When Beethoven played it for the first time to our friend Wensel Krumpholz and me, it delighted us greatly and we teased him until he repeated it.

First page from the first edition of the "Waldstein" Sonata (Sonata in C Major, Opus 53). (Library of Congress)

Passing the door of Prince Lichnowsky's house on my way home, I went in to tell him of this new and glorious composition of Beethoven's.

The prince persuaded me to play it as well as I could remember it. As I recalled more and more of it he urged me to repeat it. In this way it happened that he also learned a portion of the piece.

To surprise Beethoven, the prince went to him the next day and said that he had composed something which was not at all bad. In spite of Beethoven's remark that he did not want to hear it, he sat down and to the amazement of the composer, played a goodly portion of the Andante. Beethoven was greatly angered, and this is the reason why I never again heard Beethoven play.

Beethoven's temperament made it necessary for him to find new living quarters frequently. He asked Ries if he could find something "on a large square or on the Bastei." He wanted to work where there was good light, good air, and a pleasant view.

Ries soon found lodgings for the composer in the Pasqualati house on the Mölkerbastei. Baron Pasqualati was the physician of Empress Maria Theresa. From his rooms on the fourth floor, Beethoven could look over the ramparts (Bastei) of old Vienna and see the hazy mountains in the distance. Today the Ringstrasse has taken the place of the ramparts that once were used in the defense of the inner city. A barbershop, shoe repair shop, and other shops are now on the ground floor of the once proud Pasqualati house.

Beethoven lived in the Pasqualati house periodically. One of his pianos is still there, and his rooms are preserved as a small museum.

Many houses in Vienna display historical plaques to indicate that Beethoven lived there. He was far from an ideal tenant. The Viennese today still refer to him with hushed voices, as being *schwierig* (difficult), as though he might overhear and be offended.

Beethoven conceded that he was a clumsy fellow. When he moved around in a room he might upset a chair, stumble over anything that happened to be in the way, or knock over a glass of wine while reaching for the salt.

His dress varied from careless to elegant—the latter if he were in love at the moment with a young lady on whom he hoped to make a good impression. In his later years he was extremely careless in his dress.

"He walked with quick steps, was rather stocky, dressed in modish white socks, light trousers, and a long blue frock coat with brass buttons," one of his pupils recalled. "His white scarf was sometimes tied in a most artistic manner, sometimes carelessly. His back pockets were always filled with sketchbooks and a carpenter's pencil. With his hands behind his back, he would hurry along, then would suddenly stop and write in his book."

Beethoven must have been a very untidy tenant, for, in the heat of composing, he might walk over to a pitcher

The Pasqualati house (left), where Beethoven enjoyed the view over the bastions of the old city of Vienna. (H. J. Gimpel)

The piano Beethoven played in his rooms at the Pasqualati house on the Mölkerbastei. (H. J. Gimpel)

of water and pour it over his head to cool off. The water would cascade down his hair, splash off his broad shoulders, and finally come to rest in placid pools on the floor. It would soon seep through the ceiling, much to the distress of the tenants and the landlord.

Perhaps because of his deafness, Beethoven did not realize how loudly he pounded on the piano or stamped his feet on the floor. In any case, the noise soon made him unwelcome as a near neighbor. Since he often worked late at night and was up early in the morning, the other tenants could be assured of not getting enough sleep. As a result, the great Ludwig van Beethoven was often given notice to seek quarters elsewhere.

During these busy years of composing, Beethoven's music so filled his life and thoughts that he paid little attention to such minor trivialities as eating, resting, or even coming in out of the rain. One day in a restaurant he sat at a table and ordered his meal. During the unusually long time it took the waiter to arrive, he started to jot down notes in his ever handy sketchbook. He became so absorbed in his work that when the waiter finally did come, Beethoven, thinking he had already eaten, asked for the check. Ferdinand Ries told of another incident.

Beethoven was often extremely violent. One day when we were eating our noonday meal at the Swan Inn the waiter brought him the wrong dish.

Beethoven hardly had spoken a few words about the matter when the waiter answered back in a curt manner. Beethoven seized the dish (it was a mess of lungs with plenty of gravy) and threw it at the waiter's head.

The poor fellow had an armful of other dishes and could not help himself. The gravy ran down his face. He and Beethoven screamed and vituperated while all the other guests roared with laughter. Finally, Beethoven himself was overcome with the comicality of the situation. The waiter wanted to protest, but could not, for he was kept busy licking from his chops the gravy that ran down his face while he made the most ridiculous grimaces.

As a friend and pupil of Beethoven's, Ries had plenty of opportunities to observe the music master in moments both sublime and ridiculous. Beethoven's greatness more than compensated for his many human failings.

In his behavior Beethoven was awkward and helpless. His uncouth movements were often destitute of all grace. He seldom took anything into his hands without dropping and breaking it. Thus he frequently knocked his inkwell into the pianoforte that stood near the side of his writing table. No piece of furniture was safe from him, least of all a costly piece. Everything was overturned, soiled,

H

and destroyed. It is hard to comprehend how he
ever accomplished so much as to shave himself, even
considering the number of cuts on his cheeks.

On the whole, he was a thoroughly good and
kind man, on whom his moods and impetuousness
played shabby tricks. He would have forgiven
anybody, no matter how grievously he had in-
jured him or whatever wrong he had done him, if
he had found him in an unfortunate position.

Beethoven liked to go for a walk every day, if possible, particularly if it were summertime and he was
living in the country. He walked very fast in the city,
as though someone were chasing him. When in the countryside, his pace was slower. He often paused to take in
the beauty of the surrounding scene, drawing inspiration from the birds, the brooks, the trees, and the mountains.

One summer day, Ries went on such a walk with
Beethoven before his piano lesson.

"He had been humming all the time and sometimes
howling," Ries wrote, "always up and down, without
singing any definite notes. In answer to my question
what it was, he said, 'A theme for the last movement of
the sonata has occurred to me.'

"When we entered the room, he ran to the piano without taking off his hat. I took a seat in the corner and he
soon forgot all about me. Now he stormed for at least an
hour with the beautiful finale of the sonata. Finally he

A sketch of Beethoven walking around the ramparts of the old city of Vienna, notebook in hand. (Oesterreichische National-bibliothek, Vienna)

got up, was surprised to see me, and said, 'I can't give you a lesson today. I must do some work.' "

Karl Czerny, another piano pupil of Beethoven's who developed into a fine concert pianist, wrote of the great master's playing.

Nobody equaled him in the rapidity of his scales, double trills, and skips. His bearing while playing was masterfully quiet, noble, and beautiful, without the slightest grimace (only he bent forward low, as his deafness grew upon him). His fingers were very powerful, not long, and broadened at the tips by much playing. He told me very often indeed that he generally had to practice until after midnight in his youth.

He was also the greatest *a vista* [sight-reading] player of his time—even in score-reading. He scanned every new and unfamiliar composition like a divination. His judgment was always correct, very keen, biting, and unsparing, especially in his younger years.

Much that the world admired then, and still admires, he saw from the lofty viewpoint of his genius in an entirely different light. His playing, like his compositions, was far ahead of his time. The pianofortes of the period [until 1810], still extremely weak and imperfect, could not endure his gigantic style of performance.

As he threw himself into his work with renewed vigor, Beethoven seems to have overcome the deep depression that gripped him when he wrote his "Heiligenstadt Testament."

His good friend, Ignaz von Seyfried, described the composer as he was before he became entirely deaf.

Beethoven sometimes carried things to an extreme in his rude honesty in the case of many— mostly those who had imposed themselves upon him as protectors. The fault lay only in this, that the honest German always carried his heart on his tongue and understood everything better than how to flatter. Also because, conscious of his own merit, he would never permit himself to be made the plaything of the vain whims of those who were eager to boast of their association with the name and fame of the celebrated master. Thus he was misunderstood only by those who had not the patience to get acquainted with the apparent eccentric.

When he composed *Fidelio*, the oratorio *Christ on the Mount of Olives*, the symphonies in E-flat, C Minor, and F, the pianoforte concertos in C Minor and G Major, and the Violin Concerto in D, we were living in the same house. Since we were each carrying on a bachelor's apartment, we dined at the same restaurant, where we chatted away many an unforgettable hour in the confidential intimacy of colleagues. Beethoven was then merry, ready for any jest, happy, full of life, witty, and not seldom satirical.

Beethoven spent the year 1805, for the most part, composing his opera *Fidelio*, Opus 72. Even though this was a busy, productive year, he never seemed too occupied to fall in love with one of his pupils.

Countess Josephine Deym, a talented lady of great and noble character, took piano lessons from Beethoven almost every day. It was unusual for the composer to spend so much time with one of his pupils. Josephine's sisters, Charlotte and Therese von Brunswick, were worried about the apparent love affair between Beethoven and their recently widowed sister. Beethoven wrote to Josephine, explaining that he had tried with determination not to fall in love with her. He also wrote, "Long, long, of long duration may our love last, for it is so noble, so firmly founded upon mutual regard and friendship."

While his love for Josephine blossomed, so did Beethoven's opera *Fidelio*. To what extent his feelings of fidelity toward Josephine found their way into the opera will never be known.

As Beethoven was completing *Fidelio*, Napoleon was heading toward Vienna. The French army swarmed along the Danube, and Ulm was taken on October 20,

1805. Ten days later, the enemy legions poured into Salzburg.

Panic-stricken, the aristocracy of Vienna hurriedly packed up their valuables and left the capital. Beethoven remained behind with the lower-class and middle-class inhabitants who could not afford to leave. His wealthy patrons, the music lovers on whom his livelihood depended, had gone. His beloved Josephine too had left. Forced to flee with her children, she went to her family home in Martonvásár, and later to Budapest.

By November 10, dust rose in clouds in the suburbs of Vienna, stirred up by the legions of French soldiers, their horses, and the wheels of their artillery. By the thirteenth, French cavalry and regiments of infantry led by marshals Joachim Murat and Jean Lannes marched into the streets of the city with bands blaring and banners waving. Napoleon moved into the huge Schönbrunn palace from which the imperial family had fled a few days before. His marshals and generals found comfortable lodging in the fine houses of the aristocracy, claimed as the spoils of victory.

Beethoven's opera *Fidelio*, originally entitled *Leonore*, had an unfortunate premiere. The French officers who crowded the theater stalls found the music as strange as the language in which it was sung. The orchestra, which had practiced the new work insufficiently, played it poorly, and the woodwinds took wild stabs at the difficult notes, with disastrous results.

Title page of the opera Fidelio, Opus 72. (Oesterreichische Nationalbibliothek, Vienna)

Even the renowned soprano Anna Milder found her music difficult to sing. Later she "had severe struggles with Beethoven the music master about the unbeautiful, unsingable passages, unsuited to her voice, in the adagio of the air in E Major—but all in vain. Finally, in 1814, she declared that she would never sing the air again in its original form."

In the music periodical of Leipzig, the opera was referred to as "the oddest among the odd products of last month," and mention was made that it was received very coldly. When the second and third performances were presented before the coldest audience of all—rows and rows of empty seats—the opera closed.

With little to cheer him, Beethoven welcomed a tender letter written in Budapest by his dear Josephine.

"The closer relationship with you, dear Beethoven, these winter months, has left impressions in my heart that neither time nor circumstances will erase. Are you happy or sad?"

He would truthfully have to admit that the reception of *Fidelio* had left him very sad indeed.

At the pleading of his friends, Beethoven finally consented to shorten the opera and rewrite many of the passages. In addition to major cuts, he reworked one of the choruses ten times and revised one of the songs eighteen times. The overture was rewritten four times, and there are now three *Leonore* overtures and one called *Fidelio*. In 1814, the opera finally reached its present successful form. It is little wonder that Beethoven wrote only one opera.

Fidelio was one of Beethoven's *Sorgenkinder* (sorrow children).

"Of all my children," he said shortly before he died, "this one cost me the worst birth pangs. Even though it brought me the most sorrow, it is the one that is most dear to me."

SEVEN

"It Is a Pity I Do Not Understand the Art of War as Well as the Art of Music"

After the first performance of *Fidelio*, Beethoven was disheartened at its reception, but he plunged into his work with undaunted vigor. Count Andreas Rasumovsky, the Russian ambassador in Vienna, had commissioned him to write three quartets. They were to be played by the talented musicians the count maintained in his palace to entertain his guests.

In the spring of 1806, Beethoven was hard at work composing the quartets. He gladly received commissions to write music, for he needed the money.

"His circumstances are none of the best at present," Stephan von Breuning wrote. "Since his opera, owing to the intrigue of his enemies, was performed but seldom, it therefore yielded him nothing."

Instead of taking his usual summer sojourn in the

117

country, Beethoven climbed into a coach for a trip to Hungary. There he spent many happy days with the von Brunswicks at their huge family estate, Martonvásár. The beautiful and adoring sisters Josephine (Pepi) and Therese (Tesi) lavished their attentions on him.

Pepi, a pretty widow of twenty-six, seemed more infatuated with Beethoven than ever. She was certainly much more attractive and mature than the young girl who seven years before had played one of his trios for him in Vienna.

"The dear immortal Ludwig van Beethoven was very friendly, and as polite as he could be. He placed me at his out-of-tune piano, and I began. I played valiantly and sang the accompaniment for cello and violin," she recalled of that day.

The wonderful days and evenings at Martonvásár passed all too soon in a pleasant summer interlude. In this atmosphere, Beethoven wrote the Piano Sonata in F Minor, Opus 57—the *Appassionata*—and much of his felicitous Fourth Symphony, Opus 60. The *Appassionata* was later dedicated to Franz, the brother of Pepi and Tesi. In spite of Pepi's adoration for him, Beethoven's affection for Tesi seemed to grow during that idyllic summer.

In September, Beethoven traveled to Troppau in Silesia, now a part of Czechoslovakia, to visit Prince Lichnowsky. During this visit, Beethoven and the prince had a serious misunderstanding. Prince Lichnowsky tried to coax Beethoven to play for his guests, a group of French officers. Beethoven repeatedly refused, and the prince jokingly threatened him with arrest. The composer did not think the joke was very funny and immediately left the house without as much as a farewell.

The incident did little to endear the French to Beethoven. Their armies seemed to be constantly threatening, invading, and destroying. When he heard of Napoleon's victory at the battle of Jena in October, he remarked: "It is a pity I do not understand the art of war as well as I do the art of music. If I did, I certainly would conquer him."

Some men rise above others like hills above the plains. A very few tower above the rest like mountain peaks, in the rarefied atmosphere of greatness. Looking from one such peak to another, Beethoven could see Napoleon's greatness, but he never questioned for a moment that his genius surpassed that of Napoleon.

When Beethoven returned to Vienna in November, he had completed the three Rasumovsky quartets, Opus 59, and his Piano Concerto in G Major, Opus 58. In spite of the confusion created by the French troops quartered in the city and in the countryside, he managed to complete, by the end of the year, a number of other important works: his Fourth Symphony, in B-flat Major; a concerto for violin and orchestra; the *Leonore* Overture no. 3; and other miscellaneous compositions for orchestra and piano.

Beethoven's increased productivity imposed a greater demand on his time in correcting proofs from the publishers. The number of errors finally drowned out his patience, and he described the mistakes found in one proofreading task as "swarming in like fish in the sea." Many of his letters are filled with explosive language berating the stupidity of copiers, printers, and publishers. It apparently did not occur to him that his difficult manuscripts were often at fault.

In the summer of 1807, Beethoven again journeyed to Baden and Heiligenstadt, two of his favorite retreats. In the autumn he moved to Eisenstadt, where his Mass in C, Opus 86, was first performed.

During this time, Beethoven was working on his great Fifth Symphony, Opus 67. He had started composing parts of the symphony in 1805, and finished toward the end of 1807. Destined to become one of the world's most cherished orchestral compositions, this symphony remained unheard until December, 1808. Today its mystery, beauty, and dynamic force appeal to music audiences everywhere. Like many other compositions of Beethoven's, however, his Fifth Symphony, in C Minor, had an unfortunate introduction to the world.

The notice for the concert read: "On Thursday, the twenty-second of December, Ludwig van Beethoven will have the honor to give a musical academy in the Theater-an-der-Wien. All the pieces are of his composition, are entirely new, and have not yet been heard in public."

Included in the program were his Fifth and Sixth (*Pastoral*) symphonies and his Piano Concerto no. 4 in

G Major. In spite of his increasing deafness, Beethoven was to play his concerto. It is almost inconceivable that such a concert could result, as it did, in failure, both financial and artistic.

During the rehearsal of the Fifth Symphony, Beethoven was forced to stop the orchestra numerous times. When he tactlessly berated the musicians, they refused to play at all under his baton. Banished from the rehearsal, he listened from an anteroom. His hands behind his back, he paced back and forth. To say that the orchestra failed to do justice to the music is a gross understatement. They bungled their parts with little regret.

Beethoven was not infallible as he sat down to play his piano concerto. When he played a repeat that he had agreed to skip, it threw the orchestra completely off. Later the woodwinds tooted out boldly in a false entrance. The composer leaped up from his piano seat.

"Stop—stop! That will not do! Badly played! Again —again!"

Once humiliated, the musicians cared little whether or not they played the right notes. The concert performance of the music could best be described as a bad rehearsal.

To top off the instrumental disasters, Anna Milder refused to sing in the program. Beethoven had quarreled with her before the performance, and an inexperienced singer had to be substituted. The young girl was so frightened that she could not utter a sound. A glass of wine was administered to give her courage. Her aria, however, when finally sung, was too much Bacchus and not quite enough Beethoven.

Why the Viennese stayed away from the concert in such large numbers is not hard to understand. The poor could not afford to go, and many of the more affluent were feeling the pinch of the war reparations imposed by France. The Russian Count Vielhorsky recalled sitting in one of the orchestra stalls in lonesome solitude. Beethoven acknowledged the ripple of applause and gave the count a "personal little bow—half friendly and half ironic."

The meager box-office returns were disheartening. Artistically, the concert fared little better. The music critics and Beethoven's many enemies among the musicians made the most of the unfortunate performance. The composer was discouraged and embittered. To have his music so poorly presented, without sufficient preparation and rehearsal, was a crushing blow. He felt alone, and his deafness made him mistrust even those who tried to befriend him.

Beethoven was in a mood to consider seriously an offer for a permanent position made to him in October. It would pay well and he could leave his financial troubles in Vienna behind. Napoleon's youngest brother, Jerome Bonaparte, the new spendthrift King of Westphalia, asked him to serve as *Kapellmeister* to the court of Cassel. He was to have been handsomely paid and would have had nothing to do but play occasionally for the king and conduct his chamber concerts.

Learning of this, Countess Anna Marie Erdödy urged Archduke Rudolph, Prince Lobkovitz, and Prince Ferdinand Kinsky to counter this offer with a better one that might keep Beethoven in Vienna. In February, 1809, they agreed upon an annual payment of 4,000 gulden (about $1,200), to be shared among the three wealthy patrons. Beethoven gladly accepted their offer.

As it turned out, the arrangement was not as satisfactory as expected. Accepting the appointment as Jerome's *Kapellmeister*, however, would have been more disastrous. Jerome's reign as King of Westphalia was not destined to last any longer than Napoleon's dominance over Europe. Jerome spent his money with the wild abandon typical of men who have never had the inconvenience of earning any. His treasury was soon emptied. His crown, worn through the generosity of his brother Napoleon, was removed from his head too late to save the Westphalians from his folly.

In any case, Beethoven would not have been happy as *Kapellmeister* at the court of Cassel. Each day he was growing progressively more hard of hearing. It was difficult for him to conduct an orchestra, and his career as a concert pianist had come to an end. Composing was the last door open to him for serving his art.

As an orchestra director, Beethoven had many shortcomings, although no one could know better than he how to interpret his own music.

I

The publication *Cäcilia* reported :

Our master could not be presented as a model in respect to conducting, and the orchestra always had to have a care not to be led astray by its mentor. He had ears only for his composition and was ceaselessly occupied by manifold gesticulations to indicate the desired expression. He often made a downbeat for an accent in the wrong place. He used to suggest a *diminuendo* by crouching down more and more, and at *pianissimo* he would almost creep under the podium.

When the volume of sound grew, he rose up as if out of a stage trapdoor, and with the entrance of the power of the orchestra he would stand upon his toes almost as big as a giant. Waving his arms, he seemed about to soar upward to the skies. Everything about him was active; not a bit of his body was idle. The man was like perpetual motion. He did not belong to those capricious composers whom no orchestra in the world can satisfy. At times he was altogether too considerate and did not even repeat passages that went badly at rehearsal. "It will go better next time," he would say.

He was very particular about expression, the delicate nuances, the equable distribution of light and shade, as well as an effective *tempo rubato*. Without vexation he would discuss them with the individual players. When he then observed that the players entered into his intentions and played together with increasing ardor inspired by the magical power of his creations, his face would be transfigured with joy. All his features beamed pleasure and satisfaction, a pleased smile would play on his lips, and a thundering *"Bravi tutti!"* rewarded the successful achievement.

The out-of-doors always brought to Beethoven an exhilaration that drawing rooms and candlelight failed to inspire.

"My bad hearing does not trouble me here. In the country, every tree seems to talk to me, saying, 'Holy! Holy!' In the forest is enchantment, which expresses all things—sweet peace in the forest. Almighty, I am happy in the woods. Every tree has a voice through Thee. O God, what glory in such a wooded place!

"On the heights is peace—peace to serve Thee. How glad I am once again to be able to wander in forest and thicket, among the trees, the green things, and the rocks. No mortal can love the country as I do—for woods and trees and rocks return the echo a man desires."

Charles Neate, a British pianist, emphasized how much Beethoven drew upon nature for joy and inspiration.

"Nature was almost meat and drink to him. He seemed positively to exist upon it."

Years after he wrote his Sixth Symphony the deaf composer walked in the country with his secretary and biographer, Anton Schindler. During the walk, Schindler

Beethoven walks among the woods and fields, from which he drew constant inspiration. (Library of Congress)

related, "Beethoven constantly stopped and let his gaze roam happily over the landscape. Then, seating himself on a tuft of grass and letting his body rest against an elm, he asked me if any yellowhammers could be heard in the trees. I assured him that around us all was quite still.

"Turning to me he said: 'Here I composed the Scene by the Brook. The yellowhammers up there, the nightingales, the quails and cuckoos round about, composed with me.'"

This was the Second Movement of Beethoven's Sixth Symphony, the *Pastoral*, Opus 68. Hector Berlioz described this movement.

"We are reclining in the tall grass in a clearing by the woods, listening to the gurgling of a gentle brook. Wrapped in a dreamy mood, our thoughts drift away into the distant woods from whose mysterious depths the voice of the cuckoo is heard, softly calling."

Beethoven always felt that music should be an abstract art and should not be used to describe the physical, external objects around him. He hoped that others would realize that through his music he was describing the emotion created by nature and not the objects of nature themselves. A note at the top of his manuscript of the *Pastoral* Symphony read: "More an expression of feeling than tone painting."

The five movements of his *Pastoral* Symphony are appropriately described as "Serene Impressions Awakened by Arrival in the Country; Scene by the Brook; A

Merry Gathering of Country Folk; The Thunderstorm; Shepherd's Song—Glad and Thankful Feelings after the Storm."

At times it seems regrettable that many of Beethoven's great musical creations are listed only by such unimaginative designations as opus numbers, yet his music is infinite in meaning. It is written for whatever is within the listener himself. Each person is free to imagine his own scene and may have a different impression every time he hears a particular selection. Beethoven liked to feel that his creations were free of rigid images. If a specific idea were expressed in music, it would be like a butterfly set in cement, a bird frozen in flight, a fantasy in chains.

Beethoven believed that his music said many things to many people. Perhaps part of his greatness is that he leaves to his listeners the joy of adding that extra something that each one must provide from within himself.

As the years passed, Beethoven needed someone to show him love, someone to care about him. One day he wrote to a friend, Baron Ignaz von Gleichenstein, about Doctor Malfatti's dog, Gigons.

"If you suppose that Gigons looks for you alone, no—I too have had the joy of having him stay at my side. He ate supper close to me last night. What's more, he saw me home. In a word, he entertained me very well."

What a whimsical thought that the great master of music was so proud to have had the friendship of a dog

Sketch of a part of the "Pastoral" Symphony (Symphony No. 6 in F Major, Opus 68), from one of Beethoven's notebooks. (British Museum, London)

for a day—a friendship guileless, undemanding, and freely given.

While Beethoven was happy that Gigons seemed to like him, he never did find anyone who loved him enough to marry him. There was always some reason: he was too eccentric, too old, too poor, a commoner in love with a countess, or too busy with his music.

Many of Beethoven's titled lady friends were exceptionally gifted. Princess Maria Christiane Lichnowsky was an accomplished pianist, as were the Baroness Dorothea von Ertmann and Madame Marie Bigot. The Berlin composer and writer Johann Friedrich Reichardt visited Vienna and heard Baroness Ertmann's fine rendition of a Beethoven sonata.

"A lofty noble manner and a beautiful face full of deep feeling increased my expectation still further at the first sight of the noble lady. As she performed a great Beethoven sonata, I was surprised as never before," Reichardt wrote.

"I have never seen such power and innermost tenderness combined even in the greatest virtuosi. From the tip of each finger her soul poured forth. From her hands, both equally skillful and sure, what power and authority were brought to bear over the whole instrument. Everything that is great and beautiful in art was turned into song with ease and expression."

Beethoven seldom tolerated having his music played in a way other than as he intended. Still, when Madame Bigot played for him, he showed how considerate he could be. She played one of Beethoven's newest sonatas while he listened closely and intently. His immutable expression was enlivened only by the sparkle in his dark, deep-set eyes.

When she finished playing, Beethoven's serious face cracked into a smile as he remarked, "That is not exactly the character which I wanted to give this piece—but go right on. If it is not wholly mine, it is something better."

He was not always as considerate to musicians who played for him, as Wilhelm Rust, a musician and teacher, observed.

He is as original and singular as a man as are his compositions—usually serious, at times merry, but always satirical and bitter. On the other hand, he is also very childlike and certainly very sincere. He is a great lover of truth and in this goes too far very often, for he never flatters and therefore makes many enemies.

A good fellow once played for him, and when he had finished, Beethoven said, "You will have to play a long time before you will realize that you can do nothing."

He praised my playing, particularly in the Bach fugue, and said, "You play that well." Still, he could not omit calling my attention to two mistakes. In a scherzo I had not played the notes crisply enough and at another time I had struck one note twice instead of binding it.

Beethoven lived at a moment in history when he could shake music out of its set ways and redirect its course from the old classical school toward a fuller, freer manner of expression. Unfortunately, the zenith of his career happened to coincide with that of Napoleon. In 1809, the advance of Napoleon's army again disrupted the musical life of Vienna and scattered the patrons of music. The empress and the imperial family fled again on May 4.

To defend the city, seventeen thousand Austrian troops and civil militiamen took positions around the ramparts of the capital. By May 10, the city was besieged by Napoleon's excellent and high-spirited troops.

When Archduke Maximilian rejected the French demands to surrender the city, the French artillerymen positioned a battery of twenty howitzers on the Spittelberg heights. They opened fire during the night of the eleventh. The people ran for shelter into their cellars and toward the center of the city.

Beethoven's lodgings were well within range of the booming cannon. When the shells crashed into the Kärnthnerthor, one of the city gates, and the Wasserkunst Bastei, Beethoven fled to the house of his brother Karl on the Rauhensteingasse. Arriving safely, he spent the night sitting in the cellar with a pillow over his head, trying to protect his sensitive ears from the concussion of the bursting cannonballs.

During the night many homes went up in flames, and

the wounded citizens were carried through the streets to first-aid stations for treatment. The next day, the white flag was raised early in the afternoon as the city surrendered to the French troops.

The war did not end when the capital city fell. The battles of Aspern, Esslingen, and Wagram brought the Austrians further hardship, impoverishment, and scarcity of food. On top of all the want and suffering, there were staggering demands from the French army. Money was levied from the citizens to support the conquerors. Beethoven's music patrons had moved to distant places.

Once again, Napoleon moved into the Schönbrunn palace, and the walks through the beautiful gardens were denied to the composer. While exorbitant peace terms were being forced on the Austrians, Napoleon issued a proclamation assuring them of his goodwill as the Emperor of France, the King of Italy, and the Protector of the Confederation of the Rhine.

Somehow, through all this confusion, Beethoven managed to compose his Piano Sonata in E-flat Major, Opus 81a, the *Lebewohl* (*Farewell*) Sonata; his Piano Concerto in E-flat Major, Opus 73, the *Emperor* Concerto; and his Quartet in E-flat Major, Opus 74, the *Harp* Quartet. He also completed the Piano Sonata in F-sharp Major, Opus 78, dedicated to Therese von Brunswick, the Sonatina in G Major, Opus 79, and other works. While the world around him was in a state of disruption, his own world of music was still quite in order.

The war, which brought poverty to Beethoven, brought prosperity to his brother Johann. Johann had taken a risky venture when he bought his apothecary shop a year and a half before. The shop and house at Linz had been inherited by a lady who knew nothing about running an apothecary shop. She was anxious to dispose of her property on the Danube River, and offered it at a very favorable price.

Johann had more enthusiasm than he had cash. He managed to make the down payment to negotiate the transaction, but had difficulty in scraping together the first month's mortgage payment. Since all kinds of metal were in great demand and were bringing a high price, he sold the gratings on the windows. These did not bring enough money, however. He had noticed that all the containers in his shop were made of British tin. Tin was one of the metals that Napoleon's English blockade had placed in great demand. Johann sold all of the tin containers for a highly inflated price and replaced them with earthenware jars. In this way he managed to hang on to his new shop and home.

While most of the citizens of Austria were suffering, Johann proved himself to be a cunning opportunist. He capitalized on the enemy's occupation by selling large quantities of drugs and medicines under French army contracts. While Johann acquired a modest fortune and became a landowner, his brother Ludwig remained a highly successful, but poor, composer.

A few months before Napoleon's army occupied Vienna, Beethoven had written to Count Oppersdorf:

Best Count!

You will look at me in a false light, but necessity compelled me to sell someone else the symphony which was written for you, and another one as well [the Fifth and Sixth symphonies], but I assure you that I shall soon send the one intended for you. I hope that you have been well, and also your gracious wife, to whom I ask you to give my best wishes.

I live right under Prince Lichnowsky at Countess Erdödy's, if ever you wish to give me the honor of a visit. My circumstances are improving, without needing the help of people who would subject their friends to embarrassment. Farewell, and from time to time think of your most devoted friend.

Beethoven experienced hard times even after the fabulously productive first ten years of the nineteenth century. By the end of 1809, he had finished six symphonies, the opera *Fidelio*, fifteen piano sonatas, ten quartets, seven sonatas for two instruments, six overtures, five concertos, a septet, a ballet, an oratorio, a quintet, a mass, and numerous songs, variations, and other compositions.

The year 1810 ushered in another decade and brought his fortieth birthday, but it did not bring health or happiness.

EIGHT

"I Have Written So Much, but Earned So Little"

In the year 1810, Beethoven fell in love with a charming and talented young lady named Therese Malfatti.
Baron Ignaz von Gleichenstein, a Rhinelander and good
friend, had introduced the composer to Doctor Johann
Malfatti and his two pretty nieces, Therese and Anna.
The baron set his cap for Anna, the younger sister,
while Beethoven outdid himself with new shirts, cravats,
and material for a new suit to impress Therese. He was
head over heels in love, ecstatically happy and guided
only by his heart. He wrote to his friend:

Dear good Gleichenstein,

I am sending you 300 florins. Let me know if
you need more and how much. I'll send it right
away. Since I understand so little about these

things, as it is all so against my nature, please buy
for me linen or Bengal for shirts and at least half a
dozen cravats. Use your own good judgment, but
don't delay. You know how I need them. Today I
forwarded 300 florins to Lind [the tailor] and
thereby have followed your advice.

In another letter he wrote,

Here is the sonata I promised Therese. Since I
cannot see her today, give it to her and remember
me to all of them. I feel so happy with them all, as
though they might heal the wounds inflicted upon
my soul by wicked people. Thank you for having
taken me there. Here are fifty florins for the
neckerchiefs.

In the spring the Malfattis left for the country. Beethoven, lonely and disconsolate, wrote to Therese :

Please don't forget the pianoforte among your
occupations, or music generally. You have so beautiful a talent for it. Why not cultivate it exclu-
sively? You have so much feeling for everything
that is beautiful and good. Why will you not make
use of this in order to learn the more perfect things
in so beautiful an art?
I live very solitarily and quietly. There is still
for me a void which cannot be filled since you have

all gone and which defies even my art which has always been so faithful to me.

Although his letters to Therese lacked the ardor that one might expect from a suitor, Beethoven nevertheless prepared for his marriage by requesting his birth certificate. He wrote to Franz Wegeler:

I beg of you to secure my baptismal certificate for me. Whatever expense may attach to the matter, since you have an account with Stephan von Breuning, you can recoup yourself at once from that source. If you think it worth while to investigate the matter and make the trip from Coblenz to Bonn, charge everything to me.

One thing must be borne in mind: namely, that there was a brother born before me, also named Ludwig, who died. To fix my age beyond doubt, this brother's record must first be found, inasmuch as I already know that in this respect a mistake has been made by others. I have been said to be older than I am. Unfortunately, I lived for a time without knowing my age. I had a family register, but it has been lost, heaven knows where.

As it turned out, Beethoven's request for his birth certificate was not necessary. Therese's family would not consider the marriage of their eighteen-year-old daughter to this strange though gifted genius who was so much older than she. Baron Gleichenstein, who was by then engaged to marry Anna, had the difficult task of telling Beethoven that he could not hope to marry Therese. The composer's hopes had soared so high that it was a crushing blow.

Beethoven's disappointment did not last for long. In the month of May a new charmer entered his life. Sitting at his piano in the Pasqualati house, he had just finished playing a beautiful song about Italy, based on a theme from Goethe. He felt two gentle hands placed on his shoulders, and turned around, his face expressing surprise. When he saw an enchanting young lady standing behind him, the surprise quickly changed to pleasure.

"My name is Bettina Brentano," the lady said.

A charming twenty-five-year-old, she had come to Vienna from Frankfort to visit her brother Franz. Beethoven smiled, took her hand impulsively, and said, "I have just written a beautiful song for you. Would you like to hear it?"

Although his growing deafness prevented good voice modulation, he sang with feeling, *"Kennst du das Land?"* ("Do You Know the Land?").

Do you know the land where the citrus trees grow,
In the dark leaves the golden oranges glow?

When he finished he turned around. "Beautiful, isn't it?" Seeing her eyes shining brightly with appreciation, he added, "Marvelously beautiful."

The lovely young lady was probably included in his last remark. After repeating the song once more, he sang another on a theme from Goethe, "Dry not the tears of everlasting love." Bettina showed such glowing approval that he told her she was the kind of listener needed to inspire musicians.

"A feeling of reverential awe came over me when Herr Beethoven expressed himself with such friendly frankness, seeing that I must have appeared so utterly insignificant to him," she wrote to her friend Goethe. "I was surprised, too, for I had been told that he was unsociable and would converse with nobody.

"My family were afraid to take me to him. I had to hunt him up alone. He has three lodgings in which he conceals himself alternately—one in the country, one in the city, and the third on the Bastei. It was in the last that I found him on the fourth floor, and walked in unannounced."

Beethoven slipped into his best coat to walk home with her. He knew the way well, for Franz Brentano was a very good friend of his. Franz had married Antonie von Birkenstock, and they lived in the Birkenstock mansion overlooking the Prater, with a view of Count Rasumovsky's beautiful formal gardens.

As the two walked along, Beethoven talked about music, occasionally stopping to speak in a loud, emphatic voice with much waving of his arms. He and Bettina had a subject of great common interest—Goethe. Three years before, Bettina had visited the famous poet after she had read letters telling of his romance with her mother, Maximiliane, when she was a bride of seventeen. Bettina's curly dark hair and dark eyes reminded Goethe very much of her mother.

When Bettina impulsively visited Beethoven at the Pasqualati house, his music to Goethe's tragedy *Egmont* had been written. It was then being rehearsed for the premiere performance at the Hofburg Theater on May 24.

More than forty guests had gathered for a large dinner party when Bettina and Beethoven arrived at the Birkenstock mansion. The guests' surprise can be imagined when she walked in, hand in hand with the great Beethoven.

"After dinner," she wrote, "the entire company went up to the tower of the house to look at the view. When the rest went down and he and I were alone, he drew out his notebook. He wrote and crossed out, then said: 'My song is finished.' Leaning against the window frame, he sang it out into the air. Then he said: 'That rings true, doesn't it? It belongs to you if you like it. I wrote it for you—you inspired it. I read it in your eyes just as it was written.' "

They walked down from the tower and Beethoven went directly over to the piano. He played for a long while.

"There was a simultaneous inspiration of his pride and genius," Bettina wrote to Goethe. "When he is in such a state of exaltation his spirit produces the incomprehensible and his fingers accomplish the impossible."

That was a memorable day in Beethoven's life.

" 'A musician is also a poet,' " Bettina's letter quoting Beethoven read, 'and the magic of a pair of eyes can suddenly cause him to feel transported into a more beautiful world. In the little observation tower during the glorious May rain, that was an inspired moment for me. The most beautiful themes beamed from your eyes into my heart which one day will enchant the world.' "

To Bettina, Beethoven wrote: "Even if I do not write to you often, yet I write you a thousand times a thousand letters in my thoughts. When you write to Goethe about me, pick out all the words that express my deepest reverence and admiration for him. I am about to write him myself concerning *Egmont*, for which I have composed music, and indeed, purely out of love for his poems."

Bettina was quick to recognize Beethoven's genius, just as she had seen the greatness in Goethe. She was a girl who "collected" geniuses with a sure, appraising eye that reflected a touch of genius all her own.

Her insight into greatness is perhaps best reflected in a letter to Goethe sent from Vienna.

It is Beethoven of whom I wish to tell you, in whose presence I forgot the world and you. I am not of age, it is true, but I am not mistaken when I say what no one, perhaps, now understands and believes—he strides far ahead of the culture of humanity. And shall anyone ever overtake him? I doubt it. If only he lives until the power and the sublime enigma that lie in his soul have attained their fullest fruition, if only he reaches his loftiest goal, then surely he will lay in our hands the key to a divine knowledge that will bring true blessedness a step nearer to us.

He comes to me every day, or I go to him. For this I neglect social meetings, galleries, the theater, and even the tower of St. Stephen's. Beethoven says, "I will call for you toward evening and we will walk through the paths of Schönbrunn."

Yesterday I went with him to a glorious garden in full bloom. All the hotbeds were open and the perfume was overpowering. Beethoven stopped in the oppressive sunshine and said, "Goethe's poems have great power over me, not only because of their contents, but because of their rhythm. I am attuned and stimulated to composition by his language, which builds itself to lofty heights as if through the work of spirits and already bears within itself the mystery of the harmonies.

"From the impulse of enthusiasm I must discharge melody in all directions. I pursue it and capture it passionately. I see it flying away and disappearing in the mass of varied agitations. Now I seize upon it again with renewed passion—I cannot tear myself from it. I am impelled with hurried modulations to multiply it, and at length I conquer it. Behold, a symphony! Music, truly, is the mediator between the life of the mind and the senses."

Beethoven loved to walk and talk with Bettina. It was springtime, and she was vibrant, responsive, and understanding. They talked of music, art, poetry—many things.

"How dear to me are the few days in which we chatted or corresponded with each other," he wrote to her. "I have preserved all the little bits of paper on which your bright, dear remarks are written. I owe it to my bad ears that the best portion of these fleeting conversations is written down. Since you have gone I have had many exasperating hours in which nothing can be done. I walked about in the Schönbrunn Allee for fully three hours after you left, and on the bastion, but there was no angel who might fascinate me as you do."

Bettina wrote to Goethe in Weimar at great length, hoping to arrange a meeting between these two great men. In one of her letters she quoted Beethoven's thoughts as she remembered them.

" 'When I open my eyes I must sigh, for what I look upon is contrary to my religion, and I must despise the world that never divines that music is a greater revelation than the whole of wisdom and philosophy. Music is the wine that incites us to new creation and I am the Bacchus who presses this glorious wine for mankind and grants them intoxication of spirit. I am not at all anxious about the fate of my music. Its fate cannot be other than happy. Whoever succeeds in grasping it shall be freed from all the misery that weighs down other men.' "

In his reply, Goethe wrote: "Your letter, heartily beloved child, reached me at a happy time. You have been at great pains to picture for me a great and beautiful nature in his achievements and his strivings, his needs and the superabundance of his gifts. It has given me great pleasure to accept this picture of a truly great spirit."

Although Beethoven lost his heart to Bettina, marriage was quite another matter. She had become engaged to a young poet, Ludwig Joachim von Arnim, and they were secretly married in the spring of 1811. When they visited Weimar in September, Goethe's wife, Christiane, let Bettina know that she had worn out her welcome by attracting her husband's affections.

While Bettina, now the Baroness von Arnim, had served as the go-between for Goethe and Beethoven, it was the summer of 1812 before the two men met. In July, Beethoven had gone to the mountain resort of Teplitz. It was a popular health spa where Austrian Emperor Franz and his empress, Napoleon's Empress Marie Louise, and Prince Lichnowsky were among the many titled notables. When Goethe arrived and learned that Beethoven was there, he called on him. At first he was greatly impressed.

"Never before have I seen an artist with more power of concentration, more energy, or more inwardness," he stated.

But Goethe, still a handsome gentleman at sixty-three, was out of key with Beethoven's bluntness and bad manners. He listened to the rather disturbing vitality of this new music.

"Charming," he remarked without much enthusiasm, after Beethoven had improvised on the piano. The literary giant who had such a magnificent command of words might have been more expressive if he could have been reached by the emotional depth of Beethoven's music.

"You must know how gratifying it is to win the approval of those who understand. If you do not recognize me as your equal, who will?" Beethoven questioned. "To what beggarly mob must I play to find understanding?"

It was the nineteenth century asking a question of the eighteenth. There was no answer to bridge the gap between the genius who lived in the past and the present and the genius who was leading his art into the future.

"Goethe is too fond of the court atmosphere—far fonder than is compatible with the dignity of the poet," Beethoven wrote to his publishers.

The older, more conservative Goethe in his turn wrote, "Beethoven's talent amazes me, but unfortunately he has no self-control. He is no doubt right in finding the world detestable, but by behaving as he does he really does not make it any more pleasant for himself or for others. We must forgive him a great deal, for his hearing is getting very bad. This interferes perhaps less with his musical than with his social side. He is naturally taciturn and is becoming still more so as a result of his deafness.''

Goethe, according to his sophisticated standards, found Beethoven boorish and rude. Beethoven, at forty-one, still lacked the veneer of refined manners, and to Goethe that was unforgivable. The composer simply was not Goethe's idea of a gentleman. Even a great creative genius could not be excused such lack of polish. As a result of Goethe's attitude, Beethoven set many of the poet's words to music with little encouragement from Goethe himself.

Perhaps Goethe cannot be blamed for his neglect, because Beethoven, now almost completely deaf, found it difficult to communicate. When Beethoven left Teplitz for Karlsruhe, toward the end of July, it apparently marked the last time the two great artists would meet.

Several years later, Beethoven wrote to Goethe asking him to intercede with the Grand Duke of Weimar on his behalf, requesting that the duke subscribe to the *Missa Solemnis*.

"I have written so much, but earned so little,'' he pleaded. "A few words from you would envelop me in bliss.''

Apparently those "few words'' were too much to ask. Goethe did not even bother to answer the letter. Nevertheless, Beethoven always admired the great poet.

Looking back at his meeting with Goethe at the fashionable spa at Teplitz, Beethoven remarked, "I would have gone to my death for him then—yes, ten times over."

Even though Goethe thought Beethoven was arrogant, Emily, a ten-year-old admirer of Beethoven's, would certainly have disagreed with him. She had sent Beethoven a handmade wallet and in her girlish enthusiasm had placed him above all the old masters. As busy as Beethoven was, he wrote to her from Teplitz.

> Do not snatch from Handel, Haydn, and Mozart their laurel wreaths. These belong to them, but not yet to me. Art and learning alone raise men to the divine level. A true artist has no pride. Unfortunately, he sees that his art has no limits. He senses dimly how far he is from his goal. While he is perhaps being admired by others, he mourns that he has not yet reached the point where his better genius, like a distant sun, beckons him on. I would rather come to visit you and your family than many rich people who betray themselves with the poverty of their inner selves.

According to the research of many biographers and historians, the year 1812 was the one in which Beethoven wrote his famous "immortal beloved" letter. Whether the mysterious lady who was favored with Beethoven's undying love ever received the letter, or even knew it existed, will never be known. It was found by

Stephan von Breuning in a secret drawer of Beethoven's writing desk after the great composer died.

Beethoven had arrived at Teplitz on July 5. His letter of love was written the next morning.

On the 6th of July, in the morning

My angel, my all, my very self,

Only a few words today, and written in pencil (with your pencil). I shall not be certain of my rooms until tomorrow. What a waste of time is all this. Why this sorrow when necessity speaks? How can our love endure without sacrifices, without our demanding everything from one another? Can you change the fact that you are not wholly mine, that I am not wholly yours?

Look upon nature in all her beauty and set your heart at rest with a sense of the inevitable. Love demands all, and rightly so. Thus it is for me with you and for you with me. You are apt to forget that I must live for myself and for you as well. If we were completely united, you would feel the pain of it as little as I do.

My journey was frightful. I did not arrive here until yesterday morning at four o'clock. As there were few horses, the post coach selected another route, but what a dreadful road it was! At the stage before the last I was warned not to travel at night and about the forest, but that only made me more eager—and I was wrong. The coach broke down on the wretched road—a mere country road, a swamp. Without the two postilions I had with me I would have been stranded halfway. Esterhazy, traveling on the regular road, met with the same fate with eight horses as I did with four, yet I felt the same pleasure I always feel when I successfully overcome any difficulty.

Now, quickly I change from things external to things internal. We shall surely see each other soon. I cannot tell you now all my thoughts which during the last few days have been revolving in my mind. If our hearts were closely united, I should not have such thoughts. My heart is so full of so many things I have to say to you—Ah! there are moments when I find that speech is so inadequate.

Be cheerful—and remain forever my faithful, my only sweetheart, my all, as I am yours. The gods must send us the rest—whatever must be and shall be our fate.

Your faithful
Ludwig

In a postscript, written that evening, he continued in part:

I have just found out that letters must be posted very early on Mondays and Thursdays—the only days when mail goes from here to K. You are suffering—Ah! wherever I am, there you are also. I will arrange it so that I can live with you—what a life! But, without you—tormented by the kindness of people which I do not deserve, and little care to deserve. Humility of one man toward another pains me—and when I think of myself in relation to the universe, what am I and what is He who is the Greatest—yet this itself shows the divine in man.

However much you love me, I love you more, but do not ever conceal your thoughts from me. Good night. As I am taking the baths I must go to bed. O God—so near! so far! Is not our love truly a heavenly edifice and as firm as the vault of Heaven?

The next morning, Beethoven wrote the second postscript.

Good morning on July 7th

Even while I am still in bed my thoughts go out to you, my immortal beloved—now and then joyfully, then sadly, waiting to learn whether or not fate will take pity on us. I must live wholly with you or not at all. I have resolved to wander in distant lands, until I can fly to your arms and feel that with you I have a real home. Be calm since you know my faithfulness toward you. Never can another possess my heart, never, never. O God, why must one part from what one so loves? Yet my life in Vienna is a wretched life.

Your love has made me one of the happiest, and yet one of the unhappiest of men. At my age I need a quiet, steady life. Is that possible in our situation? My angel, I have just heard that the post goes every day and therefore I must stop so that you will receive my letter without delay. Be calm. Only by calm consideration of our existence can we attain our aim to live together. Be calm—love me—today—yesterday—how I have longed for you—you—you—my life—my all—farewell. Oh, continue to love me—never misjudge the most faithful heart

Of your beloved

L.

ever thine

ever mine

ever ours

A great mystery has surrounded this love letter. Scholars and biographers have presented exhaustive evidence to prove that one or another woman was Beethoven's "immortal beloved." Unfortunately, greatness brings with it a magnifying glass through which the masses can peer forever into the intimate details of a life.

It is hoped that this detail will always remain the personal one that Beethoven intended it to be, and that the mystery of the "immortal beloved" will always remain a mystery. Since he had so little luck in love, he deserves at least the privacy of his own heart.

NINE

"No Happiness for Thee but in Thy Art"

The year 1812 was an eventful one in the world's history as well as in Beethoven's life. This was the year when the United States declared war on Great Britain. It was also the year when the ghostly remnants of Napoleon's army staggered back from Moscow with icicles dangling from their moustaches and tinkling to the shuffle of their rag-wrapped feet.

Beethoven's life, strangely apart from these great events, was devoted to his music. In the spring he completed his Seventh Symphony, Opus 92, with its widely changing moods. This great symphony varies between brilliant exuberance and solemnity and ends with boisterous savagery as it sweeps with furious energy toward its finale. In this work, Beethoven's inner power and moods were captured for posterity.

First page of the full score of Symphony No. 7 in A Major, Opus 92. (Library of Congress)

Perhaps Beethoven's love for Amalie Sebald, whom he had met the year before, inspired his Seventh Symphony. A singer with a beautiful voice, she had completely captured his heart.

Five years after he had met Amalie, a friend wrote in her diary that "five years ago Beethoven made the acquaintance of a person, a union with whom he would have considered the greatest happiness of his life. It was not to be thought of—almost an impossibility, a mirage —nevertheless his love is now as it was on the first day." Because of this reference, Amalie is considered by some to be the lady to whom Beethoven wrote his mysterious "immortal beloved" letter.

In the fall, Beethoven traveled to Linz, where he tried to straighten out the domestic affairs of his brother Johann. A rather striking woman, Therese Obermeyer, was living with Johann and keeping house for him. Since they were not married, their relationship became a source of gossip.

Beethoven, highly incensed, arrived with the express purpose of ordering Therese out and admonishing his brother for his scandalous behavior. The composer complained to the local bishop and civil authorities, and asked that Therese be told to leave Linz. Johann did not appreciate his brother's interference with his personal affairs and, to make matters worse, he married the girl. Beethoven left in anger and later regretted his interference, for he had provoked Johann into a marriage that was to prove an unhappy one.

Johann's was not the only unfortunate marriage in the Beethoven family. Karl, Johann's redheaded older brother, had taken the plunge a few years before, in 1806. He was obliged to marry Johanna Reiss, the daughter of an upholsterer, in the month of May. Karl, their only child, was born in September. Beethoven was never skilled in handling domestic affairs of his own, let alone those of others. The net result was scorn for his two sisters-in-law and bitterness between him and his brothers.

Beethoven managed somehow to complete his Eighth Symphony, Opus 93, at Linz in 1812, amid the discords of family squabbles.

Napoleon, after languishing in Moscow amid the burned-out buildings and homes of Russia's capital, returned to Paris in the December after the retreat, looking more like an unshaven beggar than an emperor. His star was falling after he had left nations impoverished and hundreds of thousands of dead men scattered on the battlefields of Europe.

The famous composer felt the economic pinch of war severely. Austria was still on the verge of bankruptcy, and bread and survival were the primary concerns of the day. There was little money for concerts and the arts. Beethoven's generous patron, Archduke Rudolph, was hard pressed to make payments. Early in November, Prince Kinsky was killed near Prague when his saddle strap broke while he was riding. He took a nasty fall and fractured his skull. Prince Lobkovitz had lost control of his huge estate the year before. Court proceedings followed and Beethoven tried to claim what he considered legally his.

Poor management, his generosity, and his frequent moving from one lodging to another drained Beethoven's resources. Ludwig Spohr, the concertmaster of the orchestra at the Theater-an-der-Wien, missed the composer at the restaurants where they usually dined, and later asked him if he had been ill.

"My boots were," Beethoven replied, "and as I have only one pair, I was under house arrest."

While his one pair of boots was being repaired he could not leave his house. His state of mind was extremely low.

"Resignation—the most absolute and heartfelt resignation to thy fate!" he wrote in his daily journal. "Thou shouldst not live for thyself, but only for others. Henceforth there is no happiness for thee but in thy art."

The summer of 1813 found Beethoven's finances little improved. A friend in Baden, Nanette Streicher, described his poverty. "Not only did he not have a single coat, but not a whole shirt."

During this time the convent in Graz was in dire need of money and asked Beethoven to help with a fund-raising concert.

"I am just as willing now to be of service to my friends, the reverend ladies," he answered, "as I was last year without the least reward—and as I shall always be to suffering humanity as long as I breathe."

In Vienna there lived a clever inventor and mechanic, Johann Nepomuk Mälzel, who invented a mechanical trumpeter and the first metronome. His mechanical band, called the Panharmonicon, consisted of bellows, gears, and cylinders. Pins in the cylinders touched the keys of the instruments and played melodies much as a music box does. He had arranged various compositions for his Panharmonicon, and visited Beethoven to present a new idea.

In June, news had been received of Wellington's victory over the French army at Vitoria, in Spain. Mälzel suggested that Beethoven write a piece of music representing Wellington's victory, to be played on the Panharmonicon. Badly in need of money, Beethoven consented. He first wrote his arrangement for a full orchestra, and the music became known as the *Battle* Symphony, or *Wellington's Victory*, Opus 91. First performed on December 8, the composition was a tremendous success in Vienna. The highly emotional audience, which had suffered so much at Napoleon's hands, applauded wildly. The work Beethoven called "a piece of stupidity" became so popular that it relieved his financial distress and freed him for a while to write music more worthy of his genius. Presented on the same program was the premiere of Beethoven's Seventh Symphony, Opus 92.

The concert was given again four days later at University Hall for the benefit of the soldiers wounded in battle. Included in the program were two marches played by Mälzel's mechanical trumpeter with orchestral accompaniment.

After the concert, Beethoven wrote: "I esteem it my duty to thank all the honored participants in the *Akademie* given for the benefit of the sick and wounded Austrian and Bavarian soldiers who fought in the Battle of Hanau and for their demonstrated zeal on behalf of such a noble cause."

On January 2 and February 27, 1814, two very successful concerts for Beethoven's benefit were held at the Redoutensaal in the Royal Palace. The first concert included the *Battle* Symphony (also called "The Battle of Vitoria") and the singing of a bass aria. Beethoven wrote a note to Nikolaus Zmeskall, reflecting his better humor.

Dear worthy friend:

All would be well if there were but a curtain. Without it the aria will fall through. Let there be a curtain—there must be something. The aria is too dramatic, too much written for the theater, to be effective in a concert. Without a curtain or something of the sort, all of its meaning will be lost!—lost!—lost! The court will probably come. . . . Hangings!—or the aria and I will hang tomorrow!

May you fare well in the new year. I greet you warmly from my heart as in the old—with or without curtains.

Beethoven's Eighth Symphony followed the Seventh at the February concert, and the *Battle* Symphony was again played. Anton Schindler, Beethoven's good friend, secretary, and factotum, attended the concert. He recorded the success of the performance and the particular appeal of the *Battle* Symphony. The effect, he noted, was "strikingly achieved," and "heightened by the patriotic enthusiasm of those memorable days."

The concerts not only rescued Beethoven from financial distress, but sparked new interest in his opera *Fidelio*. Improvements in the score and script immediately engaged his attention. In a letter to Count von Brunswick he wrote: "My opera is going to be performed, but I am writing much of it over. I hope you are living contentedly. This is no small accomplishment. So far as I am concerned, my kingdom is in the air. Like the wind, the tones whirl around me, and often in my soul."

Beethoven found rewriting his music difficult and compared it to rebuilding the walls of an old castle. To Herr Treitschke, the stage manager of the Kärnthnerthor Theater, he wrote that to provide a new overture "will be easy because I can compose it entirely anew."

Fidelio enjoyed a success, and Beethoven's popularity and finances received another welcome lift. Johann Mälzel had given him a boost in morale and he also received an ear trumpet from the clever inventor, who thought it might help magnify sounds for Beethoven's increasingly faulty hearing. Four different ear trumpets made by Mälzel and used by Beethoven are now on display in the Beethoven-Haus in Bonn. They were of little help, however, for the great composer was becoming ever more deaf and unsociable.

The rights to the music of the *Battle* Symphony caused a dispute between the two friends that could not be resolved even by a lawsuit. They finally agreed to drop the matter, and divided the court costs.

To know Beethoven is to know many people, for he was a different kind of man in the various stages of his life. He tried to look ahead toward a newer, better life and a more eloquent and beautiful way to express himself through his music. Major General Kyd, a British music lover, once called on Beethoven. The general found him with his face lathered and his skin cut where he had started to shave. His rooms were in their usual state of disorder.

The visit got off to a disastrous start when the general sat down in a chair that crumbled under his weight. He crashed to the floor among the splintered remains. Undaunted, he offered Beethoven a hundred pounds to compose a symphony, to be performed by the Philharmonic Society of London. When the general stipulated that the symphony be written in the style of Beethoven's earlier works rather than his more recent ones,

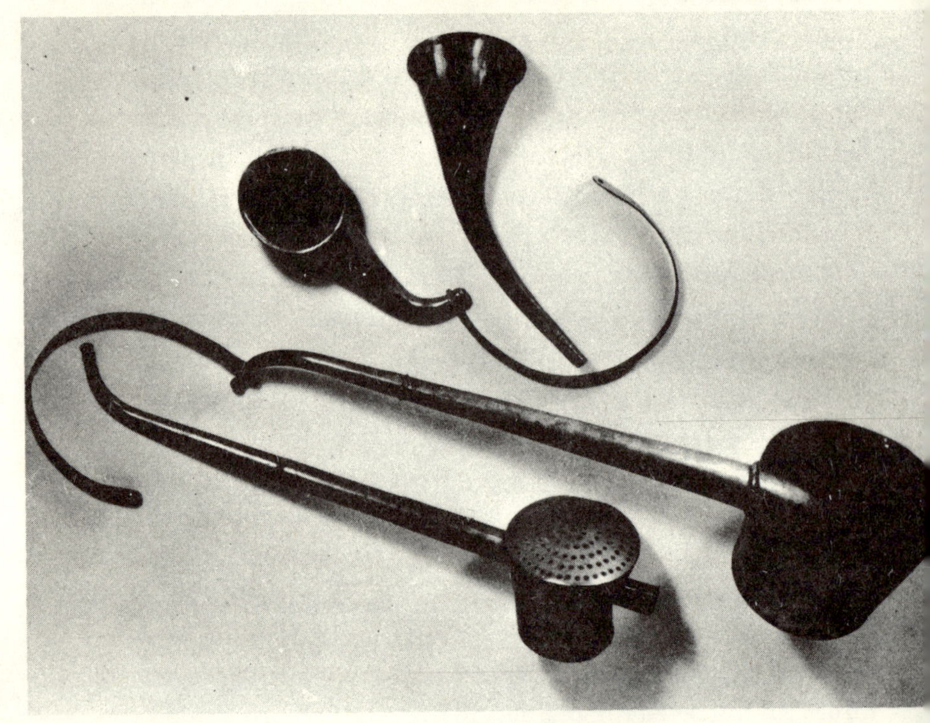

Ear trumpets made for Beethoven by Mälzel, now on display in the Beethoven-Haus. (Beethoven-Haus, Bonn)

the composer flew into a rage. The visit was quickly terminated, its purpose shattered.

The next day, while Beethoven was walking down the street with Nicolaus Simrock, one of his publishers, he saw General Kyd and remarked, "That was the man I threw downstairs yesterday."

If 1812 was a bad year for Napoleon, 1814 was even worse. He lost his campaign for the defense of France and was exiled to the island of Elba. The event was a glorious one for the countries that had suffered under the Napoleonic wars. Napoleon, the archenemy, the tyrant, and the conqueror, was at last crushed.

This same year the British burned the White House in Washington, and the Congress of Vienna brought the monarchs of the victorious European nations together in the Austrian capital.

After spending the summer in Baden, Beethoven returned to find Vienna crowded. Everyone was in a festive mood, and he helped to make it more so. The new version of his opera *Fidelio*, with the new *Fidelio* overture, was presented and enthusiastically received by the crowned heads of Europe. His cantata *The Glorious Moment* was most appropriately offered to help celebrate the happy days of peace. Needless to say, the *Battle* Symphony to Wellington's victory was received with wild acclaim time and again, as was Beethoven's Seventh Symphony.

At a concert to celebrate the birthday of the Empress of Russia on January 25, 1815, Beethoven acknowledged a round of applause. Impulsively he sat down at the piano to improvise before the royalty of Europe. These were great days for Beethoven. His financial troubles seemed to be over.

"I am exhausted by fatigue, vexation, pleasure, and joy," he wrote.

At this time, Beethoven expressed a wish that was not to be fulfilled. "May all my life be sacrificed to the sublime—may it be a sanctuary of art. Let my ear apparatus be perfected, and then I will travel! This I owe to man and the Almighty. Only thus can I develop what is locked up within me.

"The court of a prince, a little orchestra to write music for and to produce it—for the honor of the Almighty, the Eternal, the Infinite. Thus may my last years pass away, and to future humanity."

The happy scene of Vienna in the days of peace and victory continued to bring swarms of royalty from all over Europe, and the city offered a gay and elegant welcome to them. As Vienna's most honored creative artist, Beethoven held the spotlight before kings, princes, counts, and other international notables, with their beautifully gowned and jeweled ladies.

Count Rasumovsky's palatial estate was one of the busiest places, for the Russian royal family was present. The immense palace was not large enough to accommodate all the guests invited to a festival, and a wooden wing large enough for seven hundred people was built. At dawn on the first day of the new year a fire was discovered in the temporary structure and it soon raged out of control. Spreading to the main palace, it enveloped the magnificent building in flames. The count's great library and priceless art treasures were destroyed. His fortune was gone, and with it his patronage of the arts and his famous string quartet.

The disaster did not stop the Congress of Vienna, nor did it stop the whirl of concerts and social events. Another calamity, however, succeeded in destroying these happy days of peace. News quickly circulated that Napoleon had escaped from Elba and was back in France with the intention of making himself emperor once more. The Congress of Vienna ended abruptly and the royalty quickly dispersed to their own capitals, for the thunder of approaching war had all but silenced the sound of music.

The spring passed as Napoleon's military legions marched into Belgium to crush the allied armies of Europe once more. But Napoleon's disastrous defeat at Waterloo ended his dreams of conquest forever. In October he disembarked from H.M.S. *Northumberland* to his final exile at St. Helena.

At this time, Beethoven also was not faring well. He had lost his three great patrons of music. Prince Lichnowsky had died and Count Rasumovsky was ruined by the fire. Beethoven's lawsuit against Prince Kinsky's estate was finally settled and he received back payments due him. He also received money from the Lobkovitz estate and should have been relatively free of financial worries. There would soon be another financial burden for him to bear, however.

Karl, Beethoven's brother, had been ill for some time, and Beethoven had helped the family financially on numerous occasions.

In November, Karl died of tuberculosis at the age of forty-one. He left a will that had a profound effect on Beethoven's life. His nine-year-old son, Karl, was placed under the coguardianship of the boy's mother Johanna and his uncle Ludwig.

"God permit them to be harmonious for the sake of my child's welfare," Karl had requested. "This is the last wish of the dying husband and brother."

This was highly unlikely, for Beethoven was barely on speaking terms with Johanna. He considered her an unfit mother because of her infidelities and, taking a name from Mozart's opera *The Magic Flute*, he called her the Queen of the Night.

His brother's funeral had hardly taken place when Beethoven filed a petition with the Austrian civil court for sole guardianship on the grounds of Johanna's moral unsuitability. In January, 1816, the court rendered a decision in favor of Ludwig van Beethoven, and he unfortunately became his nephew Karl's legal guardian.

Now it was Beethoven's turn to demonstrate his unsuitability to raise the high-spirited young lad. The composer decided he could not possibly take the boy to live in his disorderly bachelor quarters. So, grasping Karl by the hand, he walked with him to a private boarding school in a suburb of Vienna. The school was operated by a friend, Cajetan Giannatasio del Rio. Beethoven gave Giannatasio the responsibility of prohibiting Karl's mother from seeing much of the boy. Johanna might visit her son only "in his leisure hours, without disturbing the course of his education or the domestic arrangements. She must be accompanied by a person to be appointed by the guardian or the director of the educational institution."

To take her only child away and not permit her to visit him unless accompanied stirred Johanna's wrath. She went to Beethoven to protest, and a heated quarrel resulted.

"The Queen of the Night surprised us yesterday and also delivered a veritable tirade against you," Beethoven wrote to Giannatasio. "She showed her usual impertinence and malice against me and set me back for a moment."

Beethoven went to Baden in August, 1816, and returned to Vienna in September to look after Karl, who had just recovered from a hernia operation. In taking over the project of supervising his nephew, the composer asked Nikolaus Zmeskall to help him by trying to hire satisfactory servants.

Beethoven was not an easy man to work for. His servants could not talk with him easily because he was becoming increasingly deaf. Many misunderstandings developed and grew into feuds and plots. Since Beethoven became ever more suspicious of those around him, particularly those who were not close friends, his servant problem seemed unending. His guests were asked to write down anything confidential, for he suspected his domestic help of eavesdropping. One day young Peter Simrock called on Beethoven.

"Now we can talk," the composer told Peter, "for I have given my servant five florins, a kick in the rear, and sent him to the devil."

Despite Beethoven's best efforts his home was a highly undesirable place in which to raise young Karl. The periodical *Cäcilia* described his quarters.

A truly admirable disorder prevailed in his household. Books and music were scattered in every corner. There were remnants of a cold luncheon, and sealed or half-emptied bottles. Upon a stand were the hurried sketches of a quartet or the remains of a *déjeuner*. There on the pianoforte, on scribbled paper, was the material for a glorious symphony still slumbering in embryo. Elsewhere there was a proof sheet awaiting salvation, and social and business letters covered the floor. Between the windows was a respectable loaf of strachino and a considerable ruin of a genuine Veronese salami.

Yet, despite this varied mess, our master had a habit, quite contrary to reality, of proclaiming his accuracy and love of order on all occasions with Ciceronian eloquence. Only when it became necessary and all efforts remained fruitless did he adopt a different tone, and the innocent were made to bear the blame.

"Yes, yes," he complained, "nothing is permitted to remain where I put it. Everything is moved about—everything is done to vex me!" But his servants knew the good-natured grumbler—let him growl to his heart's content. In a few minutes all would be forgotten, until another occasion brought with it a renewal of the scene.

Beethoven's problems with his servants, his frequent moving, and his nephew Karl continued to plague him.

"My household resembles a shipwreck, or threatens to," he wrote.

He often blamed his inefficient servants. "All projects concerning my nephew have foundered because of these miserable creatures."

Beethoven's chief qualifications for raising young Karl were his good intentions, his resolution to do the job well, and his love for his nephew. He had little conception, however, of what the obligation entailed in terms of day-to-day needs. It took many hours and much patience to guide the somewhat difficult lad. Valuable time had to be sacrificed on the constant trivia involved in guardianship, and the inevitable neglect of his composing cost dearly.

No one can guess the cost in terms of unwritten music. Symphonies, quartets, and sonatas had to give way to such matters as clean shirts, shoes, schoolwork, and meals for an ungrateful youth. Karl was bright enough in school, but lazy and deceitful. His poor character might be partly excused because of the mutual dislike so evident between his uncle and his mother. The suffering of all parties resulted in a dreary round of petty squabbling, court hearings, ill feeling, and misunderstanding.

"During these years," wrote Anton Schindler, "our composer, instead of writing many musical notes as had been his custom, wrote many letters referring in part to his domestic affairs, in part to the litigation, and in part to the education of his nephew. These letters are among the most deplorable testimonials to the emotional upheaval that was part of the tedious striving toward his objectives. Those of his friends who permitted themselves to be drawn into these three matters were so overwhelmed with documents and communications that they blessed the hour in which the lawsuit was brought to a conclusion."

In the summer of 1818, Beethoven left for the little country town of Mödling where he walked in the beautiful countryside, gave piano lessons to Karl, and composed very little. It was here that a young artist, August von Klöber, visited Beethoven and asked to paint his portrait. He carried a letter of introduction from one of Beethoven's friends, Joseph Valentine Dont. When the artist was given permission to paint the music master, he set to work. The two men communicated by means of a note pad and Beethoven's ear trumpet. The young man wrote his impressions of Beethoven.

After about three-quarters of an hour he grew uneasy. Following Dont's advice, I knew it was time to stop, and asked him for permission to come again tomorrow, since I lived in Mödling myself. Beethoven was very understanding and said, "Then we can meet often because I do not like to sit long. You must take a good look at Mödling, for it is very beautiful here, and as an artist you must be a lover of nature."

On my walks I met Beethoven repeatedly, and it was most interesting to see how frequently he stopped. With a sheet of music paper and a pencil stump in his hands, as if listening, he looked up and down and then scribbled notes on the paper. Dont had told me that if I met him thus I should never address him or notice him, because if I did, he would become embarrassed or disagreeable.

Once, just as I was sketching the woods, I saw him climb up a hill from the hollow that separated us. He held his broad-brimmed felt hat under his arm. When he got to the top, he threw himself down at full length under a pine tree and for a long time stared heavenwards.

Beethoven's residence in Mödling was extremely simple as, indeed, was his whole nature. When his hair was tossed by the wind there was something demoniac about him. In friendly conversation, his expression became good-natured and gentle, particularly when the conversation pleased him.

Every mood of his soul found powerful expression instantly in his features.

In the fall, Beethoven decided to place Karl in a public school in Vienna called the Academic Gymnasium. He hired a tutor to prepare the boy for enrollment, since an entrance examination was required.

Johanna, at this time, renewed her efforts to take her son away from Beethoven. After prolonged haggling and reams of legal red tape, her application was denied and Beethoven was granted permission to continue his guardianship. This was only a truce, however, in the battle over Karl.

Karl ran away to his mother's house the first week of December, and Beethoven had to call the police to get him back. Fanny Giannatasio described the upsetting scene in her diary.

> Beethoven arrived greatly excited and sought counsel and help from my father, saying that Karl had run away. I recall that on this occasion amid our expressions of sympathy he cried out in despair, "He is ashamed of me!"
>
> Never in my life shall I forget the moment when he told us that Karl was gone—had run away to his mother—and showed us a letter from Karl as proof of his vileness. To see this man suffering so—it was touching! Father took up the matter with great zeal. With all my sorrow I feel a pleasurable sensation in

the knowledge that we now are much to Beethoven
—yes, at this moment, his only refuge.

Johanna promptly appealed to the court again, setting
off another legal battle that served only to deepen resent-
ments and left a poor emotional base for any future
peace of mind for the unfortunate trio.

It is not surprising that Beethoven composed very
little of great worth during all this turmoil. He did
manage, however, to compose a number of songs, canons,
variations, and other minor works. He constantly scribbled notes, ideas, and themes in his sketchbook—poten-
tially great compositions. He considered ideas for another opera that was never written. In his sketchbook the
year before, musical notes had appeared for his Ninth
Symphony, which would not be finished for several
more years.

One of Beethoven's compositions was a lengthy
sonata, longer than any other he had previously written. He called it the *Hammerklavier* Sonata, and the
music was little understood.

Beethoven's troubles with Karl seemed to stifle the
great surge of musical inspiration that had sustained him
through other bad times. Now, when he needed the
money to help provide for Karl, he was too disturbed to
compose a great work. He even considered a trip to London, where he would conduct his compositions in spite of
his deafness.

"God help me," he wrote. "Thou seest me deserted by

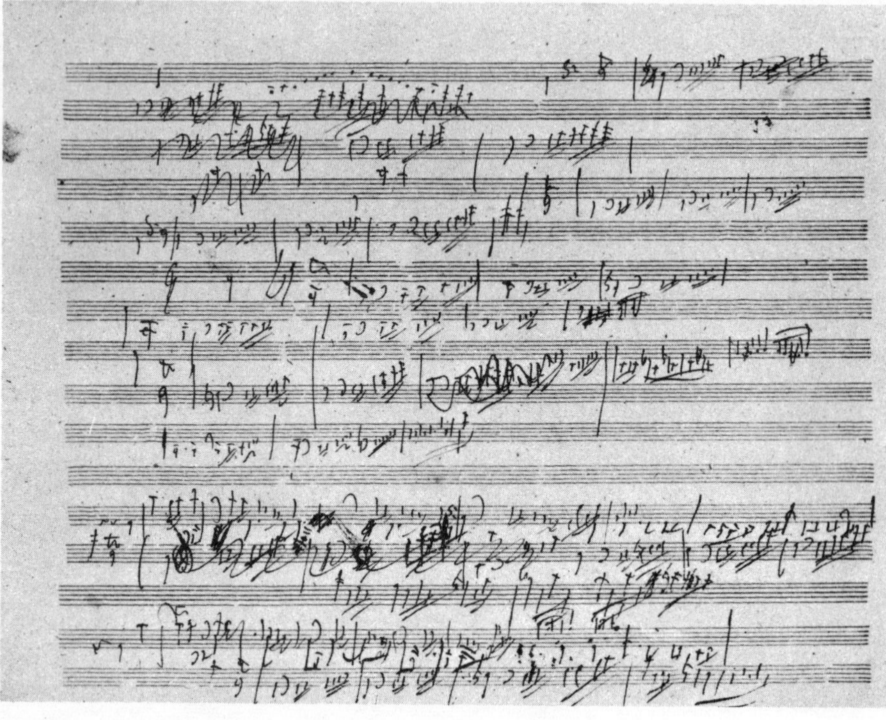

Sketches of the fugue of the "Hammerklavier" Sonata (Sonata in B-flat Major, Opus 106). These notations show how Beethoven continually reworked a theme. (Library of Congress)

all men. Hear my prayer—only for the future to be with my Karl. O harsh fate, O cruel destiny—will my unhappy condition ever end? I must work during the summer for the journey, only thus can I carry out the great task for my poor nephew. There is no salvation except to go away. Only by that can I lift myself up to the summits of my art again."

TEN

"*I No Longer Settle Down To Compose So Easily*"

The legal battle over Karl continued in the year 1819. When it was learned that the "van" before Beethoven's name did not indicate a background of nobility, as did the "von" in the various Germanic countries, the guardianship case over Karl was removed from the civil court to the city magistracy. Here a decision was given in favor of Johanna.

"The wicked woman has finally succeeded in triumphing over him," Fanny Giannatasio wrote. "Karl has been removed from his uncle's guardianship, and the wicked son returns to the source of his wickedness. I can imagine Beethoven's grief. It is said that since yesterday he has been entirely alone."

The next year—in January, 1820—the court reversed its decision in Beethoven's favor. He and court councillor Karl Peters were appointed coguardians and Karl was placed in Joseph Blöchlinger's school in the suburbs of Vienna. He was one of the older students and was described as naturally talented, but somewhat conceited because he was Beethoven's nephew.

Beethoven could now concentrate more on his music. Again, as in the year before, he chose Mödling as his summer retreat. There he took the health baths and worked on his mass, the *Missa Solemnis*. This demanding work was undertaken as a tribute to Beethoven's patron, Archduke Rudolph, who was to be enthroned as the Archbishop of Olmütz. Beethoven's great mass was over four years in the writing and he called it his most finished work. It was not completed, however, in time for the installation of the new archbishop.

Beethoven's mass had grown into a huge creation written with intense feeling, and it has moments of great ethereal beauty. While he was composing it, he withdrew into himself and appeared to have departed from the cares of this world into a higher realm of creative art—the subconscious state called a *raptus* by his friends.

"The moment he began this work," Anton Schindler recalled, "his whole nature seemed to change. He actually seemed possessed in those days, especially when he wrote the fugue and the *Benedictus*. When I recall his state of mental excitement, I must confess that I never before and never after this period of his complete forgetfulness of earth observed anything like it."

Beethoven, deeply absorbed in working on the Missa Solemnis.
(*Library of Congress*)

Schindler and a friend rode out from Vienna to visit Beethoven at Mödling. Schindler wrote of this trip:

It was four o'clock in the afternoon. Upon our arrival we learned that in the morning both servants had left. There had been a quarrel after midnight, which had disturbed all the neighbors. As a consequence of a long vigil, the servants had gone to sleep and the food that had been prepared had become unpalatable.

In the living room, behind a locked door, we heard the master singing parts of the fugue in the *Credo*——singing, howling, stamping. After we had listened a long time and were about to go away, the door opened and Beethoven stood before us with distorted features. He looked as though he had been in mortal combat with the whole host of contrapuntists——his everlasting enemies.

"Pretty doings, these!" the composer muttered. "Everybody is gone, and I have not eaten a morsel since yesterday noon."

When Beethoven was absorbed in a musical *raptus*, his detachment from the practical world around him took many peculiar turns. Professor Blasius Höfel related a story of how Beethoven got into difficulties with the police while he was staying in Baden and working on the *Missa Solemnis* during the summer of 1821.

Beethoven set out for a walk early one morning. He was wearing a shabby old coat and had not bothered to shave. Following a towpath along a canal and heedless of time and direction, he eventually lost his way. When he arrived at a small town that was strange to him, and was unable to find anyone to give him directions, he peered into the windows of several houses, trying to attract someone's attention. He succeeded all too well, for he looked like a tramp and the police were called to arrest him.

"I'm Beethoven," he explained.

"Of course you are!" the policeman countered in jest.

Because of his deafness the irony was lost on the composer.

"You're a beggar," the policeman continued. "Beethoven doesn't look like this."

Professor Höfel was having dinner in a tavern with the commissioner of police when one of the constables burst into the room.

"Herr Commissioner! We have arrested somebody who will give us no peace! He keeps shouting that he is Beethoven, but he is a ragamuffin. He wears no hat, an old coat, and has no identification."

"Lock up the tramp," the commissioner ordered. He said he would look into the matter the next morning.

Once taken into custody, Beethoven made such an uproar about being released that the police commissioner was forced to call Herr Herzog, the musical director in nearby Wiener Neustadt, to identify the man. To everyone's amazement, when the director arrived at the police station he exclaimed, "That *is* Beethoven!"

The composer was instantly released, and Herr Herzog lodged him overnight and furnished him with more respectable-looking clothes. The next day Beethoven was provided with an official carriage for his trip back to his rooms in Baden.

"Never did so great a work of art as is the *Missa Solemnis* see its creation under more adverse circumstances!" wrote Schindler.

Beethoven's letter from Vienna to Franz Brentano in November bears out this thought.

Don't consider me a shabby or thoughtless genius. For the past year up to the present I have been continually ill. During the summer I had an attack of jaundice, which lasted until the end of August. Now, thank God, things are much better. It appears that I am to be cheered up by the return of health and may live again for my art. For the past two years this has certainly not been the case, not only from poor health but also because of many other human miseries.

The Mass might have been sent before, but it had to be carefully looked through. The publishers in other countries do not get along well with my manuscripts, as I know from experience. A copy for the engraver must be examined note by note and I could not do this because of my illness. As a consequence, I have been compelled to write a considerable number of potboilers, as unfortunately I must call them.

Income from the sustaining annuity paid to Beethoven by his royal patrons had dwindled drastically and he had received little money from his music publishers. Advances paid to him by some of his publishers had put him in their debt, and illness had slowed his creative output. The expenses of raising and educating Karl added a further burden. Karl was at school and spent his vacations with his famous uncle.

Fortunately, Johann continued to prosper in the drug business and could lend his brother money. Johann had purchased an estate at Gneixendorf, but during the winter months he lived in Vienna. Gneixendorf was a name that to Beethoven sounded like "an axle, breaking."

Johann was overly proud of being a property owner. One day he called on his brother Ludwig and sent in his card, "Johann van Beethoven, landowner." Beethoven looked at it, laughed, and wrote on the back: "Ludwig van Beethoven, brain owner."

Gerhard von Breuning, the son of Stephan von Breuning, described Beethoven's strange-looking brother.

His hair was blackish-brown, hat well brushed, his clothing clean, but suggesting that of a man who wishes to be elegantly clad on Sundays. He was somewhat old-fashioned and uncouth—an effect caused by his bone structure, which was angular and unattractive. His clothing generally consisted of a blue frock coat with brass buttons, a white necktie, and light trousers. He wore linen gloves, and the fingers were so long that they folded at the ends or stuck out loosely. His hands were broad and bony.

He was not tall, but much taller than Ludwig. His nose was large and rather long. Because of the position of his eyes, it appeared as though he squinted a little with one eye. His mouth was crooked, one corner drawn upwards, giving the impression of a mocking smile. In his garb he attempted to be a well-to-do elegant, but the role did not suit his angular, bony figure. He did not in the least resemble his brother Ludwig.

The only appreciation Johann had for Beethoven's music was the income and the prestige it gave him to be known as the brother of the great composer. His wife, Therese, gained no respect for Johann in the social circles of Vienna, for she flaunted her *affaires* openly. Affluence had come to Johann, but he learned that money could not buy social graces or artistic appreciation. Once when Karl mentioned that his uncle Johann had attended a concert of chamber music, Beethoven was a little surprised and wondered why.

"He wants to acquire taste," Karl replied. "He is continually shouting 'Bravo.' "

When Beethoven had to call upon his brother for financial assistance, Johann helped to serve art in the only way he could—through his pocketbook.

Johann Friedrich Rochlitz, the music critic and editor of *Die Allgemeine Musikalische Zeitung* of Leipzig, visited Vienna in 1822. He and Franz Schubert set out for dinner together at an inn where they knew they would find Beethoven. Rochlitz reported his experience:

Beethoven sat among several acquaintances who were strangers to me. He really seemed to be in good spirits and acknowledged my greeting, but I purposely did not go over to him. I found a seat from which we could see him and, since he spoke loudly enough, we could hear nearly everything he said. It could not be called a conversation, for he spoke in a monologue at some length, and more or less at random.

Those about him contributed little, merely laughing or nodding their approval. He philosophized, or one might say politicized, after his own fashion. He spoke of England and the English, and of how both were associated in his thoughts with a splendor incomparable. He told all sorts of stories about the French, from the days of the second occupation of Vienna. For them he had no kind words. He impressed me as being a man with a rich, aggressive intellect, an unlimited, never-resting imagination.

Johann Rochlitz later proposed that Beethoven write music to Goethe's *Faust*.

"Ah," Beethoven exclaimed, "that would be a piece of work that might yield something!"

He revolved the thought in his mind for a while as he stared up at the ceiling.

"For some time I have been carrying about with me the idea of three other great works. Already I have hatched out much in connection with them, at least in my head. These I must first get rid of—two great symphonies, each different from the other, and each also different from all my other ones, and an oratorio.

"That will be a long, drawn-out affair, for I find that I no longer settle down to compose so easily. I sit and think and think, but it will not get down on paper. I dread beginning works of such magnitude. Once I have begun, however, all goes well."

Franz Schubert, the composer, idolized Beethoven, but Schubert was shy for a twenty-five-year-old, and somewhat awed by Beethoven's greatness. As a result, he admired Beethoven from a distance and unfortunately never was drawn into the circle of Beethoven's close friends. In April, Schubert had published his variations on a French song, a piano arrangement for four hands. It was dedicated to "Herr Ludwig van Beethoven by his

Worshiper and Admirer Franz Schubert." It is posterity's loss that the two great composers were destined never to know each other well.

Composing came harder for Beethoven as he tried to adjust to the ever-present silence of his deafness, and the glasses he used for his weak eyes. Yet he now could serve his art only by composing. Playing the piano before an audience and directing an orchestra were not for a deaf man. Beethoven learned this to his distress when he mounted the podium at the Kärnthnerthor Theater during a rehearsal for a benefit performance of *Fidelio*. Wielding the baton from the island of silence that enveloped him, the composer caused only confusion during the first scene. When the first duet was sung, he directed the orchestra too slowly and the musicians lagged behind the singers.

It was clear that Beethoven could not hear, and Ignaz Umlauf, the assistant director, stopped the orchestra twice. Beethoven did not know why, and no one wanted to tell him and hurt his feelings. He handed Schindler his notebook and watched as Schindler wrote: "Please do not go on—more at home."

Beethoven bounded off the stage in embarrassment.

"Quick, out of here!" he exclaimed.

He ran back to his rooms, plunged onto the sofa, and covered his face with his hands. Alone with his agony, he remained in that position until called to dinner.

"In all my experience with Beethoven," Schindler recorded, "this November day is without parallel. Before, it mattered not what disappointments or crosses misfortune brought him; he was ill-humored and depressed only for moments. He would soon be himself again, lift his head proudly, walk about with a firm step, and rule in the workshop of his genius. But he never fully recovered from the effects of this blow."

Louis Schlösser, a violinist and composer from Darmstadt, attended the performance of *Fidelio* with his friend Franz Schubert. After the finale of the opera they joined the crowd leaving the theater. Later he recalled the occasion.

> Together with us were three gentlemen to whom I paid no further attention because their backs were turned to me. As they stepped out of a lower corridor I was surprised to see all those who were streaming by toward the lobby crowding to one side, in order to give them plenty of room.
>
> Schubert very gently plucked at my sleeve and pointed with his finger to the gentleman in the middle. He turned his head at that moment so that the bright light of the lamps fell on it and I saw, familiar to me from engravings and paintings, the features of the creator of the opera I had just heard —Beethoven himself!
>
> My heart beat twice as loudly at that moment. All the things I may have said to Schubert I now no longer can recall, but I well remember that I followed the admired one and his companions

(Schindler and von Breuning, as I later discovered) like a shadow through crooked alleys and past high gable-roofed houses. I followed him until the darkness hid him from sight.

Schlösser again happened to encounter Beethoven while walking along Vienna's Kärnthnerstrasse that winter. He observed that Beethoven was unusually well dressed in "a blue frock coat with yellow buttons, impeccable white knee breeches and a vest to match. He wore a new beaver hat—as usual, on the back of his head."

When Schlösser asked his music teacher, Professor Mayseder, about Beethoven's elegant appearance, he replied: "This is not the first time that his friends have taken his old clothes during the night and laid new ones down in their place. He has not the least suspicion of what has happened and puts on whatever lies before him with complete unconcern."

It was Schlösser who passed along an insight into Beethoven's manner of composing.

"I carry my thoughts about with me for a very long time," Beethoven said, "before I set them down. My memory is so faithful to me that I am sure not to forget a theme that I have once conceived, even after years have passed.

"I make changes, reject, and rewrite until I am satisfied. Then I work it out in breadth, length, height, and depth in my head, and since I am conscious of what I want, the basic idea never leaves me. It rises, grows upward, and I hear and see the picture as a whole take shape. It stands before me as though cast in a single piece, so that all that is left is the work of writing it down. This goes quickly, if I have the time. Sometimes I have several compositions I am working on at once, but I never confuse one with the other.

"You ask where I get my ideas? That I cannot say for sure. They come to me uninvited. I could almost grasp them in my hands out in nature's openness, in the woods, during promenades, in the silence of the night, or in the early dawn. They are aroused by moods which in the poet's case are transformed into words. Mine are transformed into tones that sound, roar, and storm until at last they take shape for me as notes."

Although Beethoven's *Missa Solemnis* in D, Opus 123, was finished at the end of the year 1822, many corrections and changes had to be made. By the time it was fully completed in the spring of 1823, Beethoven had worked himself to exhaustion. The mass was first performed at St. Petersburg, Russia, in April of the next year, 1824. After Beethoven had composed the mass and three piano sonatas, there were rumors that he could write no more great works. To these rumors he responded, "Wait awhile and you'll learn that it is not true." He was soon to prove it.

Beethoven was free at last to express himself in a form that he had mastered: the symphony. A monumental work had been in his mind for six years, and ideas and themes had grown and ripened while he had struggled to complete his mass. His *Choral* Symphony now absorbed his complete attention. He worked on his themes, developed them, and wove them into greatness.

As he became more deeply engrossed in his music, Beethoven was annoyed at any disturbance and ignored the routine of his domestic affairs.

"Completely preoccupied," wrote Schindler, "he roamed through fields and pastures, sketchbook in hand, without giving a thought to the arranged hour for meals. When he returned he was repeatedly without his hat. This never happened formerly, even in the moments of highest inspiration. He filled big notebooks with notations for his new work."

Beethoven's notes for this work were compiled in the village of Hetzendorf in 1823, while he was living in rooms belonging to Baron Pronay. Problems with landlords seemed never-ending, and Beethoven suddenly decided to move to Baden. He could no longer work in the beautiful villa. The baron was much too courteous and made deep bows to Beethoven every time they met. Beethoven had once written: "The humility of man towards man—it pains me!" Schindler recalled:

The last portrait of Beethoven drawn during his lifetime. A crayon drawing by Stefan Decker, about 1824. (Historisches Museum der Stadt Wien)

This trip from Hetzendorf to Baden and the events there are among my most unusual experiences with the great eccentric. He began to reminisce over the long list of dwellings that he had already occupied there, their inconveniences, and their unpleasant aspects. Of all of them, there was only one that he had occupied that he now wanted—"but the people have declared in years past that they do not want to take me in again."

When we arrived, he requested me to proceed as a go-between to obtain the desired house, and requested that I give a promise of better order and respect for the other occupants. I was refused. Once again, as bearer of the truce, I was sent to the stronghold of the coppersmith [the landlord] with new assurances of good conduct.

This time I found a willing ear. One specific stipulation was made. In order to have the room overlooking the street, as in past years, Beethoven must provide it with window shutters. We tried in vain to learn the reason for this strange demand. Since the procurement of the shutters proved necessary for the prevention of bright sunlight on the composer's ailing eyes, however, this demand was willingly agreed to.

The two men later learned that, since Beethoven was in the habit of scribbling notes and memoranda on his shutters with a lead pencil, the owner could sell them for souvenirs. When Beethoven heard of this he burst into hearty laughter.

It was in this house that Beethoven wrote the greater part of the Ninth Symphony, Opus 125. It is also called the *Choral* Symphony, for in the fourth movement singers join the orchestra, and a grand chorus sings the happy theme from Schiller's "Ode to Joy." The symphony ends in a mood of joyful triumph.

This last symphony of Beethoven's included a number of "firsts." He introduced words and vocal music into the symphony score. He expanded the instrumentation of the symphony orchestra to include, for the first time, the piccolo and contrabassoon in the woodwinds, and the triangle, cymbals, and bass drum in the percussion section.

The Ninth Symphony was a great work, and Beethoven's longest symphony. He finally finished it in February, 1824, more than eleven years after he had composed his Eighth Symphony. The Ninth was first presented in May, at a concert which included parts of his mass, although permission had to be obtained for church music to be played in the theater. The concert was suggested by Count Moritz Lichnowsky, who asked thirty of Beethoven's friends to sign a letter requesting that the symphony first be played "in the city of its birth," Vienna.

The Kärnthnerthor hall was full. Even the bedridden Nikolaus Zmeskall, who had cut so many quill pens for Beethoven, attended, although he had to be carried in on

In a second-floor room of this house in Baden, Beethoven composed a great part of his Ninth Symphony (Symphony in D Minor, Opus 125).

In Baden, in the room where he composed his Ninth Symphony, Beethoven's piano still stands.

The house on the corner of Ungargasse and Beatrixgasse in Vienna, where Beethoven completed his Ninth Symphony. (Oesterreichische Nationalbibliothek, Vienna)

a sedan chair. The symphony was received enthusiastically, and a wild burst of applause filled the theater.
Tragically the composer was the only one there who
heard neither his great symphony nor the applause. He
stood, turning over the pages of the score, oblivious of the
standing ovation. One of the soloists, Fräulein Karoline
Unger, pulled the sleeve of his coat and turned him to
face the wildly clapping audience. It was a touching
scene, for it was obvious that Beethoven was stone-deaf.
A cruel and pitiful irony had denied the great master
composer the enjoyment of the fruits of his genius and
years of labor.

The moment of glory passed quickly, for the box-
office receipts were most disappointing. Expenses had cut
heavily into whatever financial benefit Beethoven might
have realized. Following the concert, he had dinner at
Zum Wilden Mann (To the Wild Man), where he ac-
cused his good friends Schindler and Umlauf of cheating
him.

Schuppanzigh, the great violinist; Umlauf, who directed the concert even though Beethoven was present on
the podium; and Anton Schindler all left the restaurant
and dined elsewhere. Apparently Johann van Beethoven,
jealous because Schindler handled Beethoven's business
affairs, had misinformed his brother in order to malign
Schindler.

Another concert was held later that month on a beautiful Sunday afternoon when it was much more pleasant
to stroll through the park or sit at a sidewalk café. The

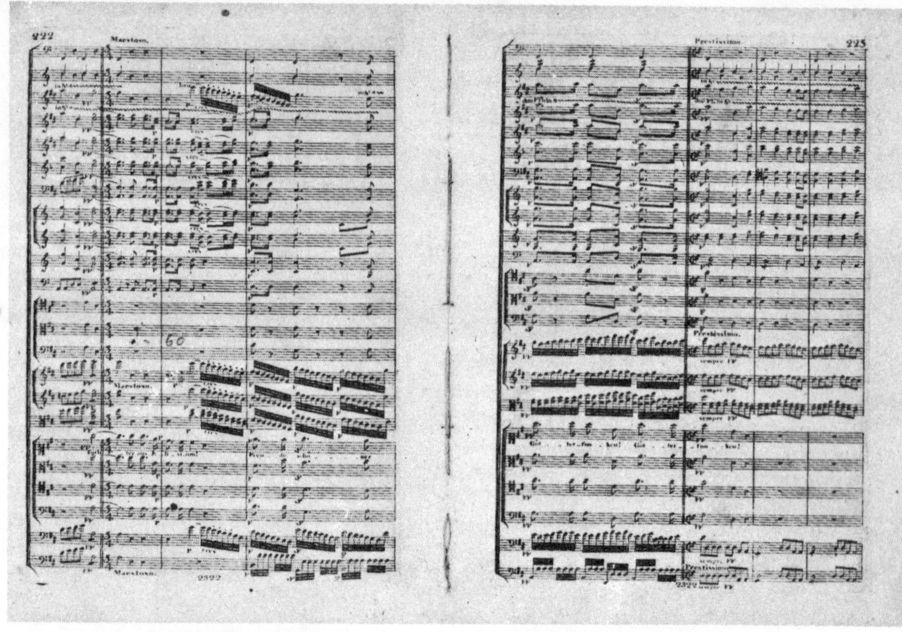

Pages from the first edition of the Ninth Symphony. (Library of Congress)

concert hall was barely half full, and instead of a profit, there was a loss. Beethoven had struggled for many years on the mass and the Ninth Symphony, only to have one more glorious moment turn into bitter disappointment.

The Ninth Symphony made little further headway as a favorite until long after its composer died. Richard Wagner finally reintroduced it. He arranged repeated performances, which were necessary before the musical world fully appreciated its greatness. The Ninth Symphony was the first of two symphonies commissioned by the Philharmonic Society of London. The Tenth Symphony would never be written, nor would Beethoven ever visit England.

After so unjustly accusing Schindler, Beethoven had to find another factotum to help look after his affairs. Karl Holz, a violinist, took on the task. He was a merry fellow whose inclination to tarry too long in the taverns caused some concern on the part of Beethoven's conservative friends. Nevertheless, he was a great help to Beethoven, who made many puns about his name. *Holz* means "wood" in German, and Beethoven called his friend such things as a "magnificent piece of mahogany" or the "best splinter from the Cross of Christ." Beethoven's letters included many puns, a form of humor that he found irresistible.

Instead of starting work on another symphony, Beethoven turned his attention to string quartets. The Russian Prince Nicolas Galitzin, who had visited Vienna and met Beethoven two years before, wrote to him from St. Petersburg requesting three new string quartets. Beethoven needed the money and besides, he had a new string quartet already in mind. It had been fourteen years since he had composed a string quartet.

The first of the quartets, in E-flat Major, Opus 127, he called *La Gaieté* and dedicated to the prince. It is full of mellow happiness and contentment, not the wild gaiety of youth.

The second and third quartets were written in 1825. The Quartet in A Minor, Opus 132, was composed as a "Holy song of thanksgiving to God of an invalid on his recovery from illness and a feeling of renewed strength."

The Cavatina of his Quartet in B-flat Major, Opus 130, was very dear to Beethoven's heart. "No piece I have ever composed has moved me so deeply. When I remember the emotions it aroused, it always brings tears to my eyes."

As originally composed, the B-flat Major String Quartet was the longest of the three written for the prince. It included a Grosse Fuge that took twenty minutes to play. When Beethoven's friends convinced him that it was too lengthy in its original form, he composed a Rondo as a finale to replace the fugue. The Rondo is written in a lighter mood than the rest of the quartet.

Beethoven's Quartet in C-sharp Minor, Opus 131, was completed the next year in July. It has a quality of mystery and ethereal peace, and in places is full of intense emotion. This quartet is one of Beethoven's great

Original manuscript of the Presto from the String Quartet in B-flat Major, Opus 130. (Library of Congress, Whittall Foundation Collection)

masterpieces. When he sent it to the publishers, Schott and Sons, he could not resist his own brand of humor.

"Put together from stolen odds and ends," he wrote on the manuscript.

The publishers sent an indignant letter to Beethoven, reminding him that he had promised an entirely new work.

Beethoven had his private laugh and replied, "That was only a joke! Don't worry, the quartet is brand-new."

Richard Wagner later called the Scherzo of this quartet the "*chef d'oeuvre* of all music." The String Quartet in F Major, Opus 135, completed at Gneixendorf in October, was his last quartet. Light and brief, it lacks the depth of the four previous ones.

In places, Beethoven's quartets were difficult to play. During a rehearsal of one of them, Schuppanzigh, playing first violin, complained of a passage that was almost impossible to perform.

"I can't think about your miserable violin when I am speaking to my God!" Beethoven exclaimed.

The composer was no more considerate of singers when he wrote vocal parts that were almost out of the normal voice range. Karoline Unger and Henriette Sontag pleaded with Beethoven to change some of the notes in the solo parts of the *Choral* Symphony. He listened to their complaints about the high sustained notes they were compelled to sing, but he would not change his work. Fräulein Unger called him "a tyrant over all the vocal organs." Annoyed at his refusal, she said to Fräulein Sontag, "Well, then we must go on torturing ourselves."

Growing older, in poor health, almost stone-deaf, and with his eyes weakening, Beethoven nevertheless retained the heart of a lion and a kinglike disdain for human limitations. In one way he had changed: he no longer laughed when people wept over his music. Now he too permitted the tears to flow when music from his pen sounded a lonely echo in his heart.

ELEVEN

"*From This World of Delusion into the Realm of Truth*"

While Beethoven was living in the magic realm of his music, the world immediately around him seemed always to involve unimportant domestic details. Ignaz von Seyfried, *Kapellmeister* at the Theater-an-der-Wien, once described one of the composer's typical days, which had changed little through the years.

From the first sunbeam to dinner (at noon), the whole morning was spent in writing his music down. The rest of the day was given over to thought and putting his ideas in order. The last mouthful had scarcely entered his lips when, unless he had no longer excursion in mind, he began his usual promenade.

He hurried on the double-quick a couple of times

around the city as though he were being prodded. Whether it rained, snowed, hailed, or the thermometer registered sixteen degrees, whether the north wind puffed his cheeks out and blew his icy breath across Bohemia's frontiers, the thunder roared, the lightning's zigzag pierced the air, a gale howled, or Phoebus' heat rays fell directly on his head—what difference did all this make to the dedicated one who carried his God in his own heart and for whose spirit, in the very midst of the elements' uproar, the mild springtide of paradise was blooming?

Beethoven's nephew was completely different from his industrious uncle. The conscientious composer found it difficult to understand a young man who seemed to have little ambition and who was content to live as a loafer.

Karl was nineteen years of age and had been attending the University of Vienna. It was a shock to his uncle when the young man decided that he wanted to enter the army instead. In the spring of 1825, he began his studies at the Polytechnic Institute, and visited Beethoven in Baden that summer, when there were no classes.

While the two were in Baden, Beethoven tried to keep Karl out of mischief by having him write letters and run errands. Beethoven had learned that Karl had spent far too much time in poolrooms and dance halls in Vienna. He had borrowed money, and his morals were questionable. The tangle of deceit, suspicion, and bitter quarreling grew progressively worse as the months went by.

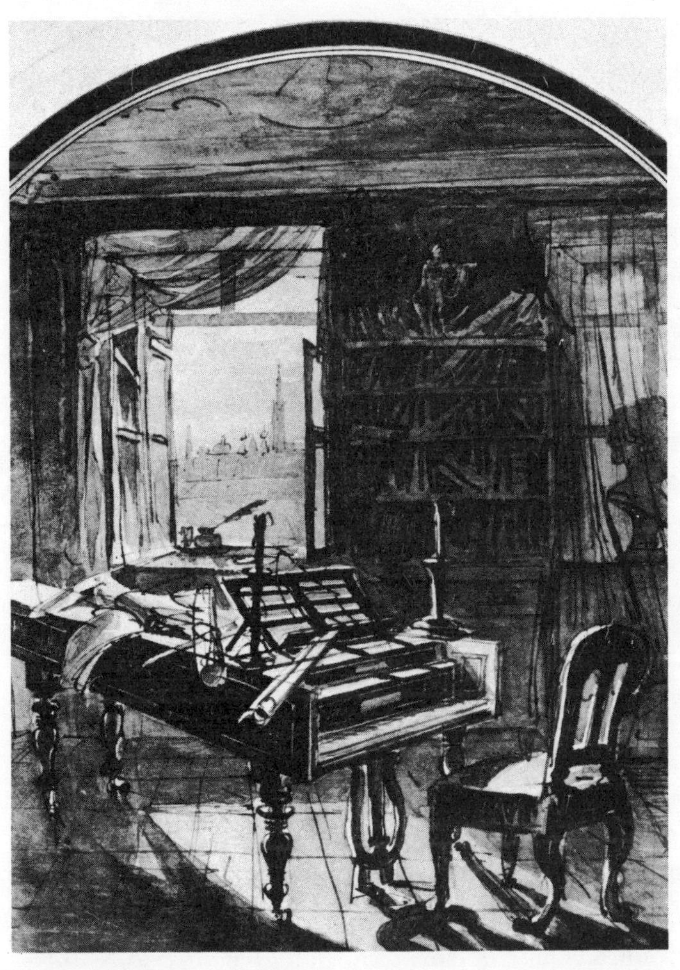

Beethoven's room in the Schwarzspanierhaus, *in Vienna. (Oester-reichische Nationalbibliothek, Vienna)*

"My heart has suffered too much from your sly behavior," Beethoven complained.

After spending the summer months in Baden, Beethoven returned to Vienna where he found lodgings at the *Schwarzspanierhaus* (Black Spaniard's House) . This was to be the last of his many residences during the stormy course of his domestic life.

Beethoven still deeply loved his nephew. Karl, however, did not return his love. He pretended to care for his uncle only when it was to his advantage. In a letter to one of his friends he ungratefully referred to his uncle as "the old fool." When Karl disappeared for days at a time, Beethoven was distracted beyond reason, but he always forgave the lad. At one such time he wrote a note to Karl.

Do not make a move that might make you unhappy and would shorten my life. I did not get to sleep until three o'clock, for I coughed all night long. I feel most cordial toward you and am convinced that you will soon cease to misjudge me. It is thus that I judge your conduct of yesterday. I expect you at one o'clock for sure. Do not give me cause for further worry and apprehension.

There followed a long series of stormy and bitter quarrels. Karl continued to mix with bad company and to go into debt by gambling, deliberately hurting his uncle. The next summer, in July, Karl threatened to take his life. He attempted to carry out his threat, though unsuccessfully.

In the secluded countryside that Beethoven loved so well, near Baden, Karl shot himself with a pair of pistols. The insecure young man apparently had a poor aim, and the bullets did not enter his head but wounded him in the forehead. A man driving a team of horses nearby heard the shots, put the bleeding lad in his wagon, and took him all the way to his mother's house in Vienna.

The effect on Beethoven was devastating; the shock to him was indescribable. "He resembled a broken old man of seventy," Schindler noted.

Prohibited from visiting Karl, Beethoven inquired about his condition through Karl Holz. In a sullen mood, his nephew responded: "What is done is done. I no longer want to be tormented with reproaches and complaints."

The von Breunings were close neighbors of Beethoven's, and Frau von Breuning asked if Karl was dead.

"No," Beethoven replied, "it was a glancing shot. He lives, and there is hope he will be saved. But the disgrace he has brought upon me! And I loved him so."

Karl threatened to tear off his bandages if Beethoven's name was mentioned. When questioned by the police, he remarked that his uncle tormented him too much and that he became worse because his uncle wanted him to be better.

Beethoven's brother, Johann, had often invited him to visit his estate at Gneixendorf. Beethoven now decided to accept while Karl was recovering from his self-inflicted wound. The composer, however, had to complete the final corrections in the manuscript copy of his Ninth Symphony before leaving Vienna.

When Beethoven and his nephew reached Gneixendorf at the end of September, they walked through the town. It consisted of one narrow, rough dirt road running between the little huts on either side. Gneixendorf lacked the charm of most of the other little villages strung along the banks of the Danube.

The pair soon arrived at Wasserhof, Johann's four-hundred-acre estate situated on a plateau near the Danube River. On the estate were two fine large houses. Most of the land was leased to tenant farmers, but boorish Johann could not play the part of a country squire.

The monotony of the almost treeless terrain was relieved by a view of the Danube River in the distance.

"The scenes which I am viewing," Beethoven wrote, "remind me somewhat of the Rhine country which I so greatly long to see again, having left there in my early youth."

There was little for Karl to do in this dull rural community, but he often visited the nearby town of Krems. His friends there were soldiers stationed nearby, and they amused themselves in a billiard parlor and a theater. When Karl's visits to the town became longer and longer, Beethoven tried to confine him to the estate.

Beethoven walked in the peaceful countryside and, as always, drew inspiration from the out-of-doors. When he returned to his room, he composed from the notes made in his sketchbook. Johann's servants were amused when Beethoven began stamping time, and talking and humming loudly to himself while he was composing. On his deaf ears the effect was completely lost, but to the servants it was hilariously comical. Johann's cook, who had the additional task of making up Beethoven's bed, surrendered herself completely to giggling and laughing over the composer's antics.

One of the workers in Johann's vineyard, Michael Krenn, was assigned to serve as Beethoven's valet—a task that would try the skill and tact of the finest "gentleman's gentleman." He proved to be the only person Beethoven trusted in that peculiar household. Though as much amused as the other servants, Krenn controlled himself until he could rush off to a safe distance and laugh to his heart's content.

"At half-past five he was up and at his table, beating time with his hands and feet, singing, humming, writing," Krenn wrote. "At half-past seven was the family breakfast. Directly after breakfast he hurried out of doors, where he sauntered about the fields, calling out and waving his hands. Walking now very slowly and then very fast, he would suddenly stand still and write in a notebook. At half-past twelve, he came into the house to dinner. After dinner he went to his own room till three or so. Then he would go again into the fields till about sunset. At half-past seven he came to supper, and then went to his room, where he wrote till ten—and so to bed."

The farmers in the area considered Beethoven a bit deranged. More than once his shouting and the waving of his arms startled the oxen pulling a plow, causing them to balk and plunge in fright. The genius in a *raptus* was too much for the local peasants to comprehend.

While Beethoven's feet stumbled along rural paths and over furrows of ploughed earth, his mind was exalted. How could these peasants appreciate what Beethoven was creating when many of the sophisticated critics of his day were not quite sure how to judge this new music?

It was at Wasserhof that Beethoven composed his String Quartet in F Major and a finale for the Quartet in B-flat Major, written to replace the Grosse Fuge finale. The Quartet in F Major was his last complete composition.

At Wasserhof the relationship between Beethoven and his sister-in-law Therese was at best very cool. Beethoven had asked that Johann make out his will in favor of Karl and cut Therese out of it as the heir to his estate. A quarrel arose because of this ridiculous demand, but some of the bickering came to an end when Therese left for Vienna.

Karl's prolonged idleness became a matter of concern. He was destined for a career in the army and was to report as soon as his head wound had healed. Beethoven decided to leave Wasserhof, even though Karl tried to persuade him to stay. He was reluctant to leave his indolent way of life.

Departing Wasserhof under less than cordial terms,

Beethoven and Karl started out on the first of December for Vienna. It was a raw, damp, frosty morning and they bounced along the country roads in an open carriage. Beethoven's light clothing was unsuited for that time of the year and by evening he was suffering from exposure to the chilly weather.

He and Karl spent that night in a village tavern in an unheated, drafty room. During the night, Beethoven contracted a persistent cough, chills, and fever. By morning he was so weak he had to be hoisted to his seat in the open carriage that he referred to as "the devil's most wretched vehicle."

Already seriously ill, Beethoven endured another long day of exposure to the penetrating cold. By the time the horse-drawn carriage lurched to a stop in front of the *Schwarzspanierhaus* he was in critical condition. When three days had passed without improvement, Karl notified Holz, who immediately found a physician.

Doctor Andreas Wawruch treated the composer and he rallied for a short while before jaundice and dropsy developed, increasing his pain. A series of four operations then became necessary to draw the excess water from his system. Beethoven's creative life was now over, but he clung to his physical life with remarkable tenacity.

In December, Beethoven received forty volumes containing the complete works of Handel. This gift from Johann Andreas Stumpff in London pleased him immensely.

"I have long wanted them," he said to his young

Beethoven during his final illness, perusing the works of Handel, whom he greatly admired. (Library of Congress)

friend, Gerhard von Breuning, "for Handel was the greatest, the ablest composer that ever lived. I can still learn from him."

It was February before Beethoven felt well enough to write a note of thanks to Stumpff.

My worthy friend! What great joy you gave me by sending the works of Handel as a present— for me a royal present. Unfortunately I have been laid up with dropsy since the third of December. You can imagine the situation this places me in! Generally I live from the proceeds of my brain, and thus I provide all things for myself and my Karl.

Unhappily, for a month and a half I have not been able to write a note. My salary suffices to pay my semiannual rent, after which there remain only a few hundred florins. It cannot yet be determined when my illness will be over and I again will be able to soar through the air on Pegasus under full sail. Doctor, surgeon, everyone must be paid.

The information that the great Beethoven was in need brought a quick response from the Philharmonic Society of London. The minutes of their meeting record that the proposal was made by Charles Neate and seconded by Latour "that this Society lend the sum of one hundred pounds of its own members to be sent through the hand

of Mr. Moscheles to some confidential friend of Beethoven, to be applied to his comforts and necessities during
his illness."

Beethoven had acquired seven valuable bank shares
that might have been used to pay his debts, but he had
put them aside as a legacy for Karl. He no longer considered them his and would not touch them. Therefore
the hundred pounds from his London friends were received with great joy. Herr Rau, a Viennese banker who
was asked to deliver the good news to the composer, wrote
to London :

I have with the greatest surprise heard from you,
who reside in London, that the universally admired
Beethoven is so dangerously ill and in want of
monetary assistance, while we, here in Vienna, are
totally ignorant of it. I went to him immediately
after reading your letter to learn about his condition and to announce the approaching relief. This
made a deep impression on him and brought forth
true expressions of gratitude. What a satisfying
sight it would have been for those who so gen-
erously assisted him to witness such a touching
scene!

I found Beethoven in a sad way—more like a
skeleton than a living being. He is suffering from
dropsy, and has already been tapped four times.
He is under the care of our clever physician

Malfatti, who unfortunately gives little hope of his recovery.

Beethoven had little strength to write of his gratitude, but Schindler, who again rallied to his aid, wrote to Ignaz Moscheles. In his letter he quoted the composer.

"Now he can again look forward to a comfortable day once in a while. Numerous times during the day he exclaimed, 'May God reward them a thousandfold.' "

Schindler had little hope that Beethoven would recover and in his letter he stated that "whatever remains of the 1,000 florins [100 pounds] we want to apply toward a respectable burial, without great fuss, in the churchyard at Döbling, where he delighted to roam."

While Beethoven was bedridden, Schindler brought almost sixty of Franz Schubert's songs to help divert the composer's still very active mind. Beethoven was delighted with the songs and amazed at their number, for he had had little chance to see any of these works before.

"Truly a divine spark dwells in Schubert," he remarked with enthusiasm. He predicted that Schubert "would become a great sensation in the world."

Beethoven wanted to see the other works of this young composer and expressed regret that he had not had the opportunity to know him better. It was too late, however. Beethoven did not have the strength to see Schubert's other works, nor the time to develop what might have been a great friendship founded in the art of

music and deep mutual respect. It was also too late for
Beethoven to show his gratitude more fully to the Philharmonic Society of London.

"May heaven very soon restore my health and I
shall prove to the generous Englishmen how greatly I
appreciate their interest in my sad fate."

In March, when the composer Johann Hummel visited
him, Beethoven praised the English people and expressed
his intention of composing "a grand overture and a
grand symphony for them."

Young Ferdinand Hiller, a pupil of Hummel's, went
with his teacher several times to visit Beethoven in
March.

"Hopeless was the picture presented by the extraordinary man when we sought him out again on the
twenty-third. It was the last time. He lay, weak and
miserable, sighing deeply. Not a word fell from his lips,
and perspiration stood out on his forehead. Hummel's
wife took her fine cambric handkerchief and dried his
face several times. Never shall I forget the grateful
glance with which he looked upon her."

With the end drawing near, Stephan von Breuning
and others who had assisted Beethoven with legal advice
decided that it was time for him to draw up a will. It was
a very short one and provided that Karl be given the
income from a trust during his life, and that the remain-
ing amount should revert to his legitimate heirs.

Beethoven read the draft of the will, struck out the

word "legitimate," and wrote "natural" in its place. Von Breuning thought the change would cause controversy, but Beethoven insisted that it meant the same thing and so it stood. Schindler called this "his last contradiction."

With great effort, Beethoven added his signature to the will and other papers. "There—now I will write no more," he said weakly. It was the last ink to flow from his pen.

The next day a number of bottles of Rhine wine, which the doctor had recommended, arrived from Mainz. Beethoven watched as Schindler placed them on the table. The composer could hardly be heard as he remarked: "Pity, pity—too late!"

That evening Beethoven went into a coma from which he never recovered. During the afternoon of March 26, 1827, von Breuning and Schindler realized that the end was near and left to select a grave site at Währing. Only Anselm Hüttenbrenner, a music dealer and friend of Schubert's, and a woman he thought was Therese van Beethoven (Johann's wife), were left with the dying composer. It was a chilly day, and snow lay on the ground in front of the *Schwarzspanierhaus*.

"After Beethoven had lain unconscious from three o'clock in the afternoon until after five, there came a flash of lightning accompanied by a violent crash of thunder, which garishly illuminated the room," Hüttenbrenner recalled. "After this unexpected phenomenon of nature, which startled me greatly, Beethoven opened his eyes and lifted his right hand. He looked up for several seconds with his fist clenched and a very serious, threatening expression.

"When he let his raised hand sink to the bed, his eyes closed part way. My right hand was under his head and my left hand rested on his chest. Not another breath— not a heartbeat more! The genius of the great master of tones fled from this world of delusion into the realm of truth." Beethoven was dead.

TWELVE

"Thus He Will Live to the End of Time"

Death, like the end of a battle, leaves so much unfinished. The morning after Beethoven's great heart stopped with the flash of lightning and the crash of thunder, von Breuning, Schindler, and Johann van Beethoven tried to put his affairs in order. They gathered in the composer's rooms to assemble his papers, and tried to locate the bank shares that he had willed to Karl.

After searching everywhere without success, Johann became impatient. He cast doubt on the honesty of von Breuning and Schindler by insinuating that the hunt was a pretense and remarked crudely that they had better produce the bank shares. Von Breuning, indignant over the unjust accusation, left the house.

In the afternoon he returned with Karl Holz, who

223

pulled a nail out of Beethoven's desk, revealing a secret drawer. Inside the drawer were the seven bank shares, Beethoven's letter to his "immortal beloved," and a small portrait of Countess Therese von Brunswick.

Beethoven's funeral took place in the afternoon on March 29, 1827. It was a mild, sunny spring day, and over twenty thousand people gathered to pay their final respects to the great composer. The crowd grew far too large to permit all the people to walk past his bier at the *Schwarzspanierhaus*, and the gates had to be closed.

It was almost impossible for the pallbearers to make their way to the church through the throngs of people who packed the streets. Many students mingled with the crowd, for the schools were closed for the occasion. The crucifer led the procession, followed by the trombonists and sixteen of Vienna's noted singers, who played and sang the *Miserere mei Deus*. Eight *Kapellmeisters* carried the richly embroidered pall. Among the torchbearers who walked on either side of the coffin was Franz Schubert, Beethoven's great admirer.

After the candlelit ceremony in the parish house of Trinity Church the casket was taken to the cemetery of Währing in a splendid ceremonial carriage drawn by four horses. At the cemetery gate Heinrich Anschütz delivered an eloquent funeral oration written by Franz Grillparzer for this occasion. In the fading light of a beautiful spring day, Anschütz' voice concluded the dramatic eulogy.

He was an artist, but a man as well. A man in every sense—in the highest. Because he withdrew from the world, they called him a misanthrope, and because he held himself aloof from sentimentality, they called him unfeeling. The finest points are those most easily blunted and bent or broken. An excess of sensitiveness avoids a show of feeling.

He fled the world because, in the whole range of his loving nature, he found no weapon to cope with it. He withdrew from mankind after he had given them his all and received nothing in return. He dwelt alone because he found no one to share his love. But to the end his heart beat warm for all men in fatherly affection. Thus he was, thus he died, thus he will live to the end of time.

You who have followed us to this place, let not your hearts be troubled. You have not lost him— you have won him. No living man enters the halls of the immortals. Not until the body has perished do their portals open. He whom you mourn stands from now onward among the great of all ages, secure forever.

Return homeward, therefore, in sorrow, yet resigned. And should you ever in times to come feel the overpowering might of his creations like an onrushing storm, when your mounting ecstasy overflows in the midst of a generation yet unborn, then remember this hour and think: We were there when they buried him, and when he died, we wept.

The sun went down, the coffin was lowered, and the torches were extinguished.

When Beethoven's nephew heard of his uncle's death, he rushed back to Vienna, but arrived too late to attend the funeral. Karl had seen his uncle for the last time in January when he left to join his infantry regiment at Iglau in Moravia.

Beethoven's grave at Währing cemetery was marked by a plain pyramid stone with one word carved on it: BEETHOVEN. With the same simplicity in which he had lived, he was committed to the ages. His grave was neglected for many years. In June, 1888, Beethoven and Franz Schubert were reburied next to each other in Vienna's Central Cemetery. Nearby are the graves of other immortals of music: Johannes Brahms, Johann Strauss, Franz Liszt, Franz Joseph Haydn, and the memorial to Mozart.

Beethoven's final great compositions after his Ninth Symphony were ethereal creations spun of deep human emotions, stardust, and galaxies, their movements speaking a higher language of time, eternity, and infinity. Many sparks of creation still glowed in his mind.

Tragically, his Tenth Symphony and other unwritten musical masterpieces were lost forever. The great music he composed still lives today, however, in homes, in concert halls, and in the hearts of millions of people all over the world. This is the truly lasting monument to the great immortal of music, Ludwig van Beethoven, master composer.

Beethoven's grave in the Währing Cemetery, near that of Schubert. (Oesterreichische Nationalbibliothek, Vienna)

Beethoven's final resting place in Vienna's Central Cemetery. (H. J. Gimpel)

CHRONOLOGY

1770   Ludwig van Beethoven born on December 16
            or 17 in Bonn, Germany, at 386 Bonngasse.
            (Today, Beethoven-Haus, 20 Bonngasse.)

1773   Death of grandfather, Ludwig van Beethoven,
            on December 24.

1774   Birth of brother Kaspar Anton Karl on April 8.

1776   Birth of brother Nicolas Johann on October 20.

1778   First public concert, at Cologne.

1780   Studied organ with Heinrich Van den Eeden.

1781   Studied music with Christian Neefe.

1781–1782   Variations for Pianoforte on a March by
            Ernst Christoph Dressler. (First published
            work, 1782.)

1782   Three piano sonatas (E-flat Major, F Minor, D
            Major). Published in 1783. "Written for and
            dedicated to my most gracious Lord the emi-

nent Archbishop and Prince of Cologne, Maximilian Friedrich."

1783   Appointed cembalist player in court orchestra.
       Rondo in A Major for Piano.

1784   Death of Elector Maximilian Friedrich. Maximilian Franz becomes new Elector of Cologne.
       Appointed assistant court organist.

1785   Took violin lessons from Franz Ries.
       Three Quartets for Piano and Strings (E-flat Major, D Major, C Major).
       Song, *"Urians Reise um die Welt,"* Opus 52. (First of eight songs.)

1786   Birth of sister, Maria Margaretha Josepha, in May.

1787   Visited Vienna and played for Mozart in April.
       Returned to Bonn because of illness of mother, in July.
       Death of mother, Maria Magdalena, July 17.
       Death of sister, Maria Margaretha Josepha, November 25.
       Moved to the Wenzelgasse.

1788   Friendship with the von Breuning family and Count Waldstein.

1789   Two Preludes for Piano or Organ, Opus 39.

1790   Franz Joseph Haydn visited Bonn in December.
       Ritterballet (eight parts).

1791   Death of Mozart on December 5.

1792   War declared between Austria and France in spring.
       Beethoven left Bonn for Vienna and began lessons with Haydn in November.

Death of father in December.

Moved to 45 Alserstrasse.

Octet for Two Oboes, Two Clarinets, Two Horns, and Two Bassoons in E-flat Major, Opus 103.

1793   Met his patrons Prince Karl Lichnowsky and Baron Gottfried von Swieten.

Lessons with Johann Schenk in August.

1794   Studied composition with Johann Georg Albrechtsberger and Antonio Salieri.

Piano Concerto No. 2 in B-flat Major, Opus 19.

Trio for Two Oboes and English Horn in C Major, Opus 87.

1795   At the Burgtheater, played his first public piano concert in Vienna, on March 29.

Played at benefit concert for Mozart's widow on March 31.

Three Trios for Piano, Violin and Violoncello, Opus 1 (E-flat Major, G Major, C Minor), dedicated to Prince Karl Lichnowsky.

Three Piano Sonatas, Opus 2 (F Minor, A Major, C Major), dedicated to Franz Joseph Haydn.

1796   Traveled with Prince Lichnowsky to Prague, Dresden, and Berlin, from February to July.

Two Sonatas for Piano and Violoncello, Opus 5 (F Major and G Minor). At Berlin, Beethoven at the piano and the court cellist played the sonatas for the King of Prussia. Dedicated to King Friedrich Wilhelm II of Prussia.

Sonata in C Major, dedicated and presented to Eleonore von Breuning.

String Trio in E-flat, Opus 3.

Quintet in E-flat Major for Piano, Oboe, Clarinet, Bassoon, and Horn, Opus 16, dedicated to
Prince Schwarzenberg.

Rondo in C Major for Piano, Opus 51.

1797–1798 Piano Sonata in D Major (four hands),
Opus 6.

Piano Sonata in E-flat, Opus 7, dedicated to
Countess Babette Keglevics.

Three String Trios (G Major, D Major, C Minor), Opus 9, dedicated to Count von Browne.

Three Piano Sonatas (C Minor, F Major, D
Major), Opus 10, dedicated to Countess von
Browne.

Trio in B-flat Major for Piano, Clarinet or Violin, and Violoncello, Opus 11, dedicated to
Countess von Thun.

Three Sonatas for Piano and Violin (D Major,
A Major, E-flat), Opus 12, dedicated to the
First *Kapellmeister* of the Imperial Court, An-
tonio Salieri.

Piano Concerto No. 1 in C Major, Opus 15, dedicated to Princess Odescalchi.

Two Piano Sonatas (G Minor, G Major), Opus
49.

1798 First sign of deafness.

1798–1799 Piano Sonata (*Pathétique*) in C Minor,
Opus 13, dedicated to Prince Karl Lichnowsky.

Two Piano Sonatas (E Major, G Major), Opus
14, dedicated to Baroness von Braun.

Six String Quartets (F Major, G Major, D Major, C Minor, A Major, B-flat Major), Opus 18. First quartets written, dedicated to Prince Lobkovitz.

1800   Met the von Brunswick family.

Summer at Unterdöbling.

Symphony No. 1 in C Major, Opus 21. Composed 1795–1800. Premiere at Royal Imperial Court Theater, April 2. Dedicated to Baron Gottfried von Swieten.

Oratorio *Christus am Ölberg* (*Christ on the Mount of Olives*), Opus 85.

Piano Concerto No. 3 in C Minor, Opus 37, dedicated to Prince Louis Ferdinand of Prussia.

Sonata in F Major for Piano and French Horn, Opus 17.

Septet in E-flat Major for Violin, Viola, French Horn, Clarinet, Bassoon, Violoncello, and Double Bass, Opus 20, dedicated to Empress Maria Theresa.

Piano Sonata in B-flat Major, Opus 22.

Rondo in G Major for Piano, Opus 51, dedicated to Countess Henriette Lichnowsky.

Sonata for Piano and Violin in A Minor, Opus 23.

Sonata for Piano and Violin in F Major, Opus 24.

Ballet *Die Geschöpfe des Prometheus* (*The Creations of Prometheus*), Opus 43, dedicated to Princess Maria Christiane Lichnowsky.

1801   Lived at Hamberger Haus.
        Summer in Hetzendorf.
        Piano Sonata in A-flat Major, Opus 26.
        Piano sonata *Quasi una Fantasia*, in E-flat Major, Opus 27, No. 1, dedicated to Princess Josephine von Liechtenstein.
        Moonlight Sonata, in C-sharp Minor, Opus 27, No. 2, dedicated to Countess Giulietta Guicciardi.
        Piano Sonata in D Major, Opus 28.
        Quintet in C Major for Two Violins, Two Violas, Violoncello, Opus 29.

1802   Summer at Heiligenstadt, where he wrote his famous "Heiligenstadt Testament."
        Symphony No. 2 in D Major, Opus 36, dedicated to Prince Karl Lichnowsky.
        Three Sonatas for Piano and Violin (A Major, C Minor, G Major), Opus 30, dedicated to Alexander I, Czar of Russia.
        Three Piano Sonatas (G Major, D Minor, E-flat Major), Opus 31.

1803   Lived at *das Rothe Haus* (the Red House) in Vienna.
        Summer in Baden and Oberdöbling (*Eroica* House).
        Sonata for Piano and Violin in A Major, Opus 47.

1804   Lived at the Pasqualati House on the Mölkerbastei.
        Summer at Hetzendorf, Baden, and Döbling.

Napoleon proclaimed Emperor of France on May 18.

Symphony No. 3 in E-flat Major (*Eroica* Symphony), Opus 55. (Composed, 1802–1804). The dedication to Napoleon and title of *Bonaparte* Symphony changed to *Eroica*, and dedicated to Prince Lobkovitz.

Piano Sonata in C Major (*Waldstein* Sonata), Opus 53, dedicated to Count Ferdinand Waldstein.

Piano Sonata in F Major, Opus 54.

Concerto in C Major for Piano, Violin, Violoncello, and Orchestra, Opus 56.

1805   French army occupied Vienna, and Napoleon moved into Schönbrunn palace on November 13.

Fidelio, Opus 72, an opera in three acts, with *Leonore Overture* No. 2 (composed 1803–05).

1806   Marriage of Karl van Beethoven to Johanna Reiss on May 25.

Birth of Beethoven's nephew, Karl, in September.

Piano Sonata in F Minor (*Appassionata* Sonata), Opus 57, dedicated to Count Franz von Brunswick.

Visited Prince Lichnowsky at Troppau in Silesia in September.

Symphony No. 4 in B-flat Major, Opus 60, dedicated to Count Franz von Oppersdorf.

Piano Concerto No. 4 in G Major, Opus 58, dedicated to Archduke Rudolph.

Three String Quartets (F Major, E Minor, C Major), Opus 59, dedicated to Count Andreas Rasumovsky.

Concerto for Violin in D Major, Opus 61, dedicated to Stephan von Breuning.

Fidelio, Opus 72. Opera revised to two acts, with *Leonore* Overture No. 3.

1807   In Baden and Heiligenstadt during July and August.

In Eisenstadt in September.

Symphony No. 5 in C Minor, Opus 67. (Beethoven conducted first performance at the Theater-an-der-Wien, December 22, 1808.)

Mass in C Major, Opus 86, dedicated to Prince Ferdinand Kinsky.

1808   Summer in Heiligenstadt with Franz Grillparzer family in the Grinzingerstrasse.

At Countess Erdödy's on Krugerstrasse in fall.

In October, offer from Jerome Bonaparte to serve as *Kapellmeister* to the court of Cassel.

Symphony No. 6 in F Major (*Pastoral* Symphony), Opus 68, dedicated to Prince Lobkovitz and Count Rasumovsky.

Sonata for Piano and Cello in A Major, Opus 69, dedicated to Baron von Gleichenstein.

Two Trios for Piano, Violin, and Violoncello (D Major, E-flat Major), Opus 70, dedicated to Countess Anna Marie Erdödy.

Fantasia for Piano, Orchestra, and Chorus in C Minor (*Choral Fantasia*), Opus 80, dedicated to His Majesty Maximilian Joseph, King of Bavaria.

1809   Annual income given to Beethoven by Archduke Rudolph, Prince Lobkovitz, and Prince Kinsky, in February.

Napoleon's troops bombarded Vienna, and Napoleon again occupied Schönbrunn palace, in May.

Piano Concerto No. 5 in E-flat Major (*Emperor* Concerto), Opus 73, dedicated to Archduke Rudolph.

String Quartet in E-flat Major (*Harp* Quartet), Opus 74, dedicated to Prince Lobkovitz.

Fantasia in G Minor for Piano, Opus 77, dedicated to Count Franz von Brunswick.

Piano Sonata in F-sharp Major, Opus 78, dedicated to Countess Therese von Brunswick.

Piano Sonatina in G Major, Opus 79.

Piano Sonata in E-flat Major (*Lebewohl* Sonata), Opus 81a.

1810   Became almost totally deaf.
Lived at Pasqualati house.
Summer in Baden.
Egmont, music to Goethe's tragedy, Opus 84.

String Quartet in F Minor (*Quartetto Serioso*), Opus 95, dedicated to Nikolaus Zmeskall.

Two Sextets in E-flat Major, Opus 71 and Opus 81b. (Earlier works, published this year.)

1811   Met Johann Nepomuk Mälzel, inventor of the metronome.
Piano Trio in B-flat Major, Opus 97.

Die Ruinen von Athen (*The Ruins of Athens*) (music to a play), Opus 113.

König Stephan, Oder Ungarns erster Wohltater (music to a play), Opus 117.

1812   Met Goethe at Teplitz in July.

Visited Linz in October.

Marriage of Johann van Beethoven and Therese Obermeyer in November.

Symphony No. 7 in A Major, Opus 92, dedicated to Count Moritz von Fries. (Beethoven conducted first performance on December 8, 1813, at University of Vienna.)

Symphony No. 8 in F Major, Opus 93.

Sonata for Piano and Violin in G Major, Opus 96.

1813   *Battle* Symphony, or *Wellington's Victory* (*Wellingtons Sieg, Oder die Schlacht bei Vitoria*), Opus 91, dedicated to the Prince Regent of England (later George IV).

1814   Napoleon exiled to Elba, in April.

Congress of Vienna convened, in September.

Lived at Bartenstein House on the Mölkerbastei.

Fidelio, Opus 72, revised for third time and new overture written for 1814 performance.

Polonaise in C Major, Opus 89, dedicated to Elizabeth Alexievna, Empress of Russia.

Piano Sonata in E Minor, Opus 90, dedicated to Count Moritz Lichnowsky.

Cantata, *Der Glorreiche Augenblick* (*The Glorious Moment*), Opus 136.

1815   Napoleon escaped from Elba in February.
        Napoleon defeated at Waterloo on June 18.
        Beethoven lived at Lamberti house.
        Summer in Baden and Mödling.
        Death of brother Karl on November 16, and be-
            ginning of lengthy lawsuits over guardianship
            of nephew.
        Two Sonatas for Piano and Violoncello (C
            Major, D Major), Opus 102, dedicated to
            Countess Anna Marie Erdödy.

1816   Became nephew Karl's legal guardian on Janu-
            ary 9.
        Lived at *zum Römischen Kaiser* (The Roman
            Emperor).
        Summer at Baden.
        Piano Sonata in A Major, Opus 101, dedicated to
            Baroness Dorothea von Ertmann.
        Song cycle "*An die ferne Geliebte*" ("To the
            Distant Beloved"), Opus 98.

1817   Lived at *Die Goldene Birne* (The Golden Pear).
        Summer at Heiligenstadt and Nussdorf.
        Ill health prevented trip to England.
        Fugue in D Major for String Quintet (Two Vio-
            lins, Two Violas, Violoncello), Opus 137.

1818   Lived at *zum grünen Baum* (The Green Tree),
            on Gärtnergasse.
        Summer at Mödling, working on *Missa Solemnis*.
            Lived at a potter's house.
        Health improved.
        Piano Sonata in B-flat Major (*Grosse Sonate für*

das Hammerklavier), Opus 106, dedicated to Archduke Rudolph of Austria.

1819 Summer at Mödling.

Court granted Karl's mother coguardianship with Leopold Nussbock in September.

1820 Appellate Court reversed decision of lower court in January, and Beethoven and Councillor Peters appointed coguardians of Karl.

Summer at Mödling.

Piano Sonata in E Major, Opus 109, dedicated to Fräulein Maximiliane Brentano.

1821 Lived on Landstrasse.

Summer at Unterdöbling.

Piano Sonata in A-flat Major, Opus 110.

1822 Met Franz Schubert.

Summer at Oberdöbling and Baden.

Piano Sonata in C Minor, Opus 111.

1823 At Hetzendorf and Baden in summer, working on Ninth Symphony.

Lived in fall at *zur Schönen Sklavia* (The Beautiful Slave).

Missa Solemnis in D Major for Orchestra, Chorus, and Solo Voices, Opus 123, (composed 1818–23). Dedicated to Archduke Rudolph of Austria, and first performed in St. Petersburg, Russia, in April, 1824.

1824 Summer at Baden.

Lived in fall at the Kletschka house on Johannesgasse and on Krügerstrasse.

Symphony No. 9 in D Minor (*Choral* Symphony), Opus 125, (composed 1817–24).

Dedicated to Friedrich Wilhelm III of Prussia and performed at Kärnthnerthor Theater in May.

String Quartet in E-flat Major, Opus 127, dedicated to Prince Nicolas Galitzin.

1825 Summer at Baden.

Moved in fall to *Schwarzspanierhaus* in Vienna, his last residence.

String Quartet in A Minor, Opus 132. String Quartet in B-flat Major, Opus 130. Both quartets dedicated to Prince Galitzin.

Grosse Fuge for String Quartet in B-flat Major, Opus 133, dedicated to Archduke Rudolph.

1826 Nephew Karl attempted suicide in July.

Visited brother's estate at Gneixendorf with Karl in September.

Became seriously ill on return trip to Vienna in December.

String Quartet in C-sharp Minor, Opus 131, dedicated to Baron von Stutterheim (July).

String Quartet in F Major, Opus 135, dedicated to Johann Wolfmayer (October).

New Finale to the String Quartet in B-flat Major, Opus 130, dedicated to Prince Galitzin (November).

1827 Beethoven died at the *Schwarzspanierhaus* on March 26.

Buried in Währing cemetery on March 29.

1888 Reburied next to Franz Schubert in Central Cemetery in Vienna.

In addition to the important works listed, Beethoven composed over two hundred songs, besides rondos, bagatelles, minuets, dances, marches, variations, and other miscellaneous music.

INDEX

243